C. J. Bartlett *British...*

Jeremy Black *...*
in ...

Anne *... the ...*

FORTHCOMING TITLES

Walter L. Arnstein *Queen Victoria*
Ian Arthurson *Henry VII*
Eugenio Biagini *Gladstone*
Peter Catterall *The Labour Party, 1918–1945*
Gregory Claeys *The French Revolution Debate in Britain*
Pauline Croft *James I*
Eveline Cruickshanks *The Glorious Revolution*
John Davis *British Politics, 1885–1939*
David Dean *Parliament and Politics in Elizabethan and Jacobean England, 1558–1614*
Susan Doran *English Foreign Policy in the Sixteenth Century*
David Eastwood *England, 1750–1850: Government and Community in the Provinces*
Colin Eldridge *The Victorians Overseas*
Richard English *The IRA*
Angus Hawkins *British Party Politics, 1852–1886*
H. S. Jones *Political Thought in Nineteenth-Century Britain*
D. E. Kennedy *The English Revolution, 1642–1649*
Carole Levin *The Reign of Elizabeth I*
W. David McIntyre *British Decolonisation*
A. P. Martinich *Thomas Hobbes*
R. C. Nash *English Foreign Trade and the World Economy, 1600–1800*
Richard Ovendale *Anglo-American Relations in the Twentieth Century*
Ian Packer *Lloyd George*
Murray Pittock *Cultural Identities in Britain and Ireland, 1685–1789*
Murray Pittock *Jacobitism*
Robin Prior and Trevor Wilson *Britain and the Impact of World War I*
Philip Rider *The Industrial Revolution*
Brian Quintrell *Government and Politics in Early Stuart England*
Stephen Roberts *Governance in England and Wales, 1603–1688*
David Scott *The British Civil Wars*
John Spellman *John Locke*
W. Stafford *John Stuart Mill*
Alan Sykes *The Radical Right in Britain*
Ann Weikel *The Elizabethan Counter-Reformation*
Ann Williams *Kingship and Government in Pre-Conquest England*
Ian Wood *Churchill*
Michael Young *Charles I*

History of Ireland

Toby Barnard *The Kingdom of Ireland, 1641–1740*
Sean Duffy *Ireland in the Middle Ages*
Alan Heesom *The Anglo-Irish Union, 1800–1922*
Hiram Morgan *Ireland in the Early Modern Periphery, 1534–1690*

History of Scotland

I. G. C. Hutchison *Scottish Politics in the Twentieth Century*
Roger Mason *Kingship and Tyranny? Scotland, 1513–1603*
John McCaffrey *Scotland in the Nineteenth Century*
John Shaw *The Political History of Eighteenth-Century Scotland*
Bruce Webster *Medieval Scotland*

History of Wales

Gareth Jones *Wales, 1700–1980: Crisis of Identity*

Please note that a sister series, *Social History in Perspective*, is now available. It covers the key topics in social, cultural and religious history.

Disraeli and Victorian Conservatism

T. A. Jenkins

First published in Great Britain 1996 by
MACMILLAN PRESS LTD
Houndmills, Basingstoke, Hampshire RG21 6XS
and London
Companies and representatives
throughout the world

A catalogue record for this book is available
from the British Library.

ISBN 0–333–64342–9 hardcover
ISBN 0–333–64343–7 paperback

First published in the United States of America 1996 by
ST. MARTIN'S PRESS, INC.,
Scholarly and Reference Division,
175 Fifth Avenue,
New York, N.Y. 10010

ISBN 0–312–16092–5

Library of Congress Cataloging-in-Publication Data
Jenkins, T. A. (Terence Andrew), 1958–
Disraeli and Victorian conservatism / T. A. Jenkins.
p.   cm. — (British history in perspective)
Includes bibliographical references and index.
ISBN 0–312–16092–5
1. Disraeli, Benjamin, Earl of Beaconsfield, 1804–1881.   2. Great
Britain—Politics and government—1837–1901.   3. Conservativism—Great
Britain—History—19th century.   4. Conservative Party (Great
Britain)—History.   I. Title.   II. Series.
DA564.B3J415   1996
941.081'092—dc20   96–7529
                                                    CIP

10   9   8   7   6   5   4   3   2   1
05   04   03   02   01   00   99   98   97   96

Printed in Hong Kong

CONTENTS

Contents

ACKNOWLEDGEMENTS

I am grateful to the House of Lords Record Office, and to the Gloucester and Somerset County Record Offices, for access to archive material in their care.

I would also like to express my appreciation of the labours by the staff of the Disraeli project, in Canada, who have thus far produced five volumes of Disraeli's complete correspondence. It is to be hoped that this project will continue to receive the support it deserves.

NOTE ON PARTY TERMINOLOGY

By the mid-1830s, the party label 'Conservative' was beginning to displace the older title of 'Tory', although contemporaries often used these party names interchangeably — as, indeed, we still do today. However, the term 'Tory' was adopted by some, at various times, to denote a political tradition founded on the defence of established institutions, like the Crown, which allegedly commanded widespread popular support. This represented a contrast to the 'Conservative' strategy, associated above all with Sir Robert Peel, which had similar objectives but sought to achieve them through an alliance between the aristocracy and the middle classes.

In 1846 the Conservative party was disastrously split over the question of the repeal of the Corn Laws. Those who opposed repeal, the bulk of the party, were sometimes labelled 'Protectionists', but they soon reverted to calling themselves Conservatives, and this is how I have chosen to describe them. The followers of Peel, who supported the repeal of the Corn Laws, are referred to as 'Peelites'.

There was no less terminological confusion on the other side of politics. At the beginning of the Victorian age, the 'party' of the left was in reality a fragile alliance of Whigs, radicals and semi-independent Irish MPs. I have used the generic term 'Liberal' to describe this alliance when referring to events after 1846. However, the older sectional labels continued to survive. For instance, contemporaries frequently described the aristocratic leaders of the Liberal party as 'Whigs', and this could also be a convenient blanket term for all moderate Liberals.

1
IMAGINATION AND POLITICS

Introduction

In the summer of 1837 a dissolution of Parliament took place — the last time that this was to be a legal requirement owing to the death of the monarch, King William IV having passed away in June. The first general election of the reign of Queen Victoria saw Benjamin Disraeli returned for the borough of Maidstone, thus securing his entry to the House of Commons at the fifth attempt, at the age of almost thirty-three. Disraeli presented himself in his election address, as 'an uncompromising Adherent to that ancient Constitution, which was once the boast of our Fathers, and is still the Blessing of their Children'. He expressed his determination to uphold the prerogative rights of the Crown, and the 'equal Privileges' of the two Houses of Parliament, which he regarded as the best means of securing for 'the great body of the Nation that unrivalled and hereditary Freedom which has been the noble consequence of our finely balanced scheme of legislative power.' In particular, Disraeli declared that he was anxious to protect the rights of the established Church of the nation, 'that illustrious Institution to which we are not less indebted for our civil than for our spiritual liberties.' Finally, he emphasised his deep concern for the landed interest, promising to 'watch with vigilant solicitude over the Fortunes of the British Farmer, because I sincerely believe that his welfare is the surest and most permanent basis of general Prosperity.' For all the elaborate language, these were impeccably orthodox sentiments for a Tory — or, to use the increasingly fashionable label, 'Conservative' — member of parliament.[1]

There was nothing in the least bit conventional, however, about the new member for Maidstone, either in terms of his personality and reputation or of his political ideas. Indeed, it would not have been easy to predict, at the dawn of the Victorian age, that within a decade Disraeli would be established as a key figure in the Conservative party, and that he would go on to become one of the party's leaders for over thirty years, remaining at the top through many vicissitudes until his death in 1881. The flamboyant, alien adventurer, that most people perceived Disraeli to be in 1837 later held the Premiership on two occasions, becoming the confidant of his sovereign and a statesman of international stature, and he ended his life as the Earl of Beaconsfield. It is certainly true, nonetheless, that nothing that Disraeli achieved in his political career was gained without a long struggle, and almost until the end his position appeared to be precarious and his legacy dubious. An extraordinary feat of imagination had been involved in the process whereby Disraeli identified himself with — and ultimately became the spokesman of — a party which overwhelmingly represented the interests of the aristocratic and landed elite. Quite clearly, the Victorian Conservative party would not have developed in the same way without him.

A young adventurer

Modern biographers of Disraeli have rightly stressed the point that the social impediments to his rise to public prominence can easily be exaggerated.[2] Born in London on 21 December 1804, Disraeli was certainly not from a poor family. Both his paternal and maternal grandfathers had been Italian Jews who had migrated to England in the mid-18th century and prospered there, one as a stockbroker, the other as a merchant. Disraeli's father, Isaac, was sufficiently comfortably off to eschew business and live the life of a gentleman of leisure, pursuing his literary interests and making a modest reputation for himself, notably through his volumes of anthology, the *Curiosities of Literature*. Later on, though not until Benjamin had reached manhood, Isaac leased a landed estate, Bradenham, in Buckinghamshire.

Disraeli's family background can therefore best be described as urban middle-class, with aspirations to gentility; if not a part of the hereditary social elite, the Disraelis were by no means sunk in obscurity. It is true that the family was of Jewish origin, but this did not necessarily constitute an impossible social handicap in early-19th century England.[3] Little is known for sure about Benjamin's upbringing, but what does emerge very clearly is that from an early age he had a pronounced sense of his differentness from other people. His obviously foreign appearance — black locks of hair, a pale complexion and dark eyes — together with his self-conscious Jewishness, help to account for Disraeli's belief that he was an outsider, and it seems likely that this was reinforced by his educational experiences. At the age of nine he was sent to an Anglican boarding school, Potticary's at Blackheath, where it is reported that Disraeli and another Jewish boy were allowed to sit at the back of the class during formal worship and also received separate lessons in Hebrew on Saturdays. It is not hard to see how this might have contributed to a sense of personal alienation from his fellow pupils. In 1817 Issac Disraeli, who had always been personally indifferent about religion, finally broke from his local synagogue and was persuaded, as a simple matter of social expediency, that it would be best to have his children brought up as Christians. Perhaps significantly, there is a suggestion that Benjamin, now almost thirteen years old, put up some resistance to his own conversion. The subsequent plan seems to have been that Benjamin should attend Winchester, one of the most prestigious public schools, but his mother, Maria, resisted this because of her fears about the brutality of life at the school. It is interesting to note, however, that Maria raised no such objections later on to her younger sons, Ralph and James, being educated there, and one cannot help wondering whether the explanation is that Benjamin had suffered badly from bullying at Potticarys. He was sent instead to another boarding school, Higham Hall in Essex, which was run by a nonconformist minister, so that ironically it was the Anglican boys, including Benjamin, who were subject to separate treatment, having to travel a long distance on Sundays to attend Church. After the summer term of 1820 he resolved not to return to Higham Hall, a decision in which the school was ready to concur, informing his parents that their son was 'of foreign and seditious mind, incapable of acquiring the spirit of the school.'[4] The young Disraeli's education appears to have been completed in his father's library, and he rejected a suggestion that he should go to Oxford University. If his political career was to a certain extent impeded by social obstacles, one has to conclude that these were partly of Disraeli's own making.

For a time Disraeli seemed destined for a career in the legal profession, working as a clerk in a solicitor's office, but he was temperamentally incapable of submitting for long to the necessary discipline and routine of office work, and he soon plunged himself into a number of risky ventures in an apparently desperate quest for instant glory and fortune. The years 1824–5 were a boom period in the London financial markets, and Disraeli became involved with speculators seeking to cash in on the mania for investment in the newly independent States of South America. Disraeli's first published works, in fact, were a series of pamphlets encouraging the public to put their money into South American mining companies. Predictably, the bubble burst and Disraeli incurred debts which were the origin of the serious financial embarrassments that plagued him for many years to come. (It is extraordinary to think that at this point he was still, legally, a minor.) In the general atmosphere of feverish speculation, though, Disraeli was undeterred from being drawn into a scheme to set up a new daily newspaper, *The Representative*, which was envisaged as a rival to *The Times*. *The Representative* was financed largely by the publisher John Murray, a friend of the Disraeli family, but it proved to be an immediate flop. Disraeli had already become disengaged from the venture by that time, amid accusations of bad faith (for reasons that are not entirely clear), but the experience provided him with useful subject matter for another project, his first novel, *Vivian Grey*, which was published anonymously in 1826. Parts of the novel sought to depict everyday life in English high society — circles in which Disraeli had never moved — and it had been cleverly 'puffed' in advance of publication by encouraging the belief that it was the work of an 'insider'. When, however, soon after the book's appearance the real identity of its author was discovered, Disraeli became the target for ferocious and abusive attacks by the reviewers.

In his impatient bid for immediate success, Disraeli had managed to leave behind him a trail of debts and bad feeling, and his only achievement was public notoriety. Everything he had done had served to harm his prospects rather than enhance them. Before reaching the age of twenty-two Disraeli suffered what was probably a nervous breakdown, and a virtually blank period of some three years were to follow during which he struggled to shake-off his mental lassitude. Only after a lengthy period of travel through the Mediterranean region and the Near East in 1830–1 (which incidentally did much to inspire his Byronic, romantic imagination) did he finally recover his health.

Socially speaking, the Benjamin Disraeli of the early 1830s was a none-too-successful novelist, renowned more than anything else for his outrageous lifestyle. Disraeli was what contemporaries called a 'dandy', an extravagant dresser moving in fairly high (but not the highest) circles in London society, and an associate of disreputable characters like Count d'Orsay and Lady Blessington. According to one description of Disraeli in this period, we find him attired in 'green velvet trousers, a canary-coloured waistcoat, low shoes, silver buckles, lace at his wrists, and his hair in ringlets.'[5] His arrogance and callous wit did not always make him popular, and he acquired the nickname of 'the Jew d'esprit'. He also caused a scandal by openly living for a time with a married woman, Henrietta Sykes. Yet in spite of his frivolous image, Disraeli's ambitions were increasingly being channelled into the pursuit of a career in politics.

Disraeli's early politics

Some idea of the intensity of Disraeli's craving for success can be gained from reading the introspective jottings contained in what is known as his 'mutilated diary'.[6] In the entry for 1833, we find the romantic declaration that 'My life has not been a happy one. Nature has given me an awful ambition and fiery passions. My life has been a struggle, with moments of rapture — a storm with dashes of moonlight.' He looked to a future in which he believed he would assail the world with renewed energy and revealed that the thing he dreaded more than anything else was the prospect of mediocrity. 'Alas I struggle from Pride. Yes it is Pride that now prompts me, not Ambition. They shall not say I have failed.' That his burning desire for fame was now driving him in the direction of politics is shown by another passage, which proved to be remarkably prophetic: 'I am only truly great in action. If ever I am placed in a truly eminent position I shall prove this. I co[ul]d rule the House of Commons, altho' there wo[ul]d be a great prejudice against me at first.'

Disraeli had already made several attempts to gain entry to the House of Commons. Early in 1832 he began to nurse the borough of Wycombe, in Buckinghamshire, on the strength of the fact that his father was now resident in the county. Both of the sitting members for the borough were Whigs, supporters of Earl Grey's government which was in the process of forcing through Parliament the Great Reform Bill; this was at least one of the reasons why Disraeli put himself forward as an independent Radical candidate, advocating the secret ballot, triennial parliaments, and greater economy in government expenditure. The sudden resignation of one of the Whig MPs prompted an unexpected by-election in June, fought on the old franchise, and at the end of the year there was a general election contested on the new £10 householder franchise. On both occasions, however, Disraeli's efforts proved unsuccessful against the entrenched Whig interest in the borough.

Following his second defeat at Wycombe, Disraeli immediately offered himself as a candidate for the county of Buckinghamshire (such switches were possible because polling did not take place in all constituencies on the same day, county contests usually being held after those for the boroughs), but here he presented himself in a very different light to the electors, claiming to be above all else a friend of the farmers committed to maintaining agricultural protection. In the event, Disraeli withdrew from the Buckinghamshire contest before polling began, owing to the entry of a stronger candidate into the field. His next attempt to find a parliamentary seat also proved abortive when, in April 1833, he issued an address to the populous London constituency of Marylebone, where a by-election was anticipated. High property values in London meant that, under the £10 householder franchise, Marylebone had a large working-class electorate, and Disraeli tailored his position to suit the borough by claiming to be an unambiguously anti-aristocratic radical. This initiative was wasted, though, as the expected vacancy did not arise after all. At the next general election, held early in 1835, Disraeli tried his luck again at Wycombe, posing as an independent Radical, although we now know that he had secretly received a subsidy from the Tory headquarters in London to encourage him to challenge the Whigs. Once again, Disraeli was defeated. However, when a by-election occurred at Taunton in the summer of 1835, Disraeli came forward for the first time as an officially recognised candidate for the Tories, and in spite of yet another defeat he was subsequently much better placed to secure his goal of a seat in the House of Commons. This he finally achieved, as we have already seen, at Maidstone in 1837.

It would be very easy simply to dismiss Disraeli's early political career as an exercise in opportunism, and in a sense this view is undeniably true. His inconsistencies are glaringly obvious, and they were commented on at the time, especially by those who suspected that — for all his professed radical sympathies when contesting Wycombe — he was really a Tory in disguise (after all, he had never faced a Tory opponent in the borough). Prior to the 1835 general election, Disraeli still had a foot in both camps, using his connections with the Earl of Durham, a leading radical, and with Lord Lyndhurst, a prominent Tory, in the hope of finding a winnable seat. Eventually, it was to be through Lyndhurst's patronage that Disraeli became firmly enrolled in the Tory ranks.

However, Disraeli's attempt to straddle radicalism and Toryism deserves more serious consideration than this, for it was not quite so absurd a position to adopt as appears to be the case at first sight. It is important to bear in mind just how fluid the political situation appeared to be in the early 1830s. The Whigs had come into office in November 1830 pledged to carry a Reform Bill, while the Tories were in disarray owing to their divisions over the question of Catholic Emancipation in 1827–30. Furthermore, once the Reform Bill was placed on the statute book the Whigs were able to go to the country at the end of 1832 and secure a crushing electoral victory, reducing the Tories to a rump of little more than 150 MPs. It was therefore reasonably open to doubt whether the Tories could ever recover from this disaster sufficiently to be able to regain power. But while it appeared possible that the Tories were finished as a party of government, the Whigs and their associates, the Radicals, were far from constituting a harmonious political grouping. A slow and often painful process of political assimilation had to occur before the Whigs and Radicals managed to form anything resembling a coherent 'Liberal' party. In the early 1830s it was not entirely unreasonable for an observer of the political scene to look upon the Radicals, with their belief in the need for more far-reaching reforms than the Whigs were prepared to offer, as the enemies rather than the friends of Earl Grey's government. Bearing in mind these considerations, Disraeli's famous remark in a letter to a family friend, Benjamin Austen, prior to his first contest at Wycombe, becomes more easily intelligible: 'I start on the high Radical interest... Toryism is worn out, and I cannot condescend to be a Whig.'[7]

Disraeli's intense dislike of the Whigs is the most intriguing aspect of his political thinking, and the most difficult to account for. It is likely that this was partly a matter of heredity: Isaac Disraeli, though he never engaged in active politics, was mildly Tory in his opinions, and the ill-fated *Representative* newspaper with which the very young Benjamin was associated through his father's friend, John Murray, had been 'Canningite' in its political allegiance. Disraeli, in other words, was probably a Tory at heart all along. Unfortunately, his long illness and subsequent foreign travels between 1826 and 1831 mean that we have no real evidence with which to judge how his political views were developing.[8] The fact that he was attracted to the Radicals rather than the Whigs may still seem rather surprising, and can probably best be explained by reference to Disraeli's romantic temperament, inspired as it was by a devotion to the memory of the great radical poet, Lord Byron. It is also relevant to note that Disraeli's closest friends in the early 1830s, Count d'Orsay and the novelist, Edward Bulwer-Lytton, were both radical in their politics.

In April 1833, shortly after his abortive Radical candidacy at Marylebone, Disraeli published a pamphlet, entitled 'What is He?', in which he sought to justify his heterogeneous political principles.[9] Disraeli's diagnosis of the problem facing post-Reform Act Britain was that its government was weak, because it was founded on no consistent principles, and that this threatened to lead to a state of chaos in which property, and ultimately civilisation itself, would be endangered. It was Disraeli's view, therefore, that 'We must either revert to the *aristocratic* principle, or we must advance to the *democratic*', and it seemed to him that the choice must be for the democratic principle. The Whigs, he argued, in forcing through their Reform Bill, had destroyed the aristocratic principle of government when they vanquished the House of Lords, using the threat of a mass creation of peers in order to oblige the upper House to submit to their will. However, in concluding that it was necessary to adopt the democratic principle if anarchy was to be avoided, Disraeli maintained that there was common ground between the Tories and the Radicals ('A Tory and a Radical, I understand; a Whig — a democratic aristocrat, I cannot comprehend'), and that it was their 'duty to coalesce.. and permit both political nicknames to merge in the common, the intelligible, and the dignified title of a National Party.' To this end, Disraeli advocated the implementation of the secret ballot and triennial parliaments, followed by an immediate dissolution of Parliament, so that a new House of Commons could be returned, 'a great majority of which would be influenced by the same wishes, and, consequently, the machine of the State would be able to proceed.'

By 1835, on the other hand, Disraeli was campaigning avowedly as a member of the Tory party, and it therefore became necessary to reconcile this fact with his earlier statement of principle in order to counter the accusations of inconsistency and opportunism levelled against him. In his address issued at the time of the Taunton by-election in June 1835, and in two subsequent letters to a Taunton solicitor, Edwards Beadon, justifying his position as an official Tory,[10] Disraeli maintained that a new national party was in fact in existence, thanks to the incompetence of the Whig government and the good sense of the people. That national party was, of course, the Tory (or, as some now preferred, Conservative) party of Sir Robert Peel, which had made substantial gains at the general election in January 1835, thus allaying the earlier fears that it had been irreparably damaged by the disasters of 1827–32. In these circumstances, Disraeli argued, there was no longer any need for democratic measures like the secret ballot and triennial parliaments, and this was why he no longer advocated them. As he asserted in the first of his long letters to Edwards Beadon:

> the Tory party is the real democratic party of this country. I hold one of the first principles of Toryism to be that Governt is instituted for the welfare of the many. This is why the Tories maintain national institutions, the objects of which are the

protection, the maintenance, the moral, civil, and religious education of the great mass of the English people...I deny that the Tories have ever opposed the genuine democratic or national spirit of the country.

Had it not been the Tories, after all, who inserted into the Great Reform Bill the Chandos clause, enfranchising £50 tenant farmers? And was it not the case, as Disraeli noted in his second letter to Beadon, that Sir Francis Burdett, the great Radical leader, had now joined the Tories?[11]

What Disraeli was gradually evolving was not simply an explanation of his political position in relation to the present situation, but a highly distinctive interpretation of the last 600 years of English history, which provided a context for understanding the present situation and, therefore, Disraeli's position in it. This historical interpretation was more fully developed in a substantial pamphlet published in December 1835, Disraeli's 'Vindication of the English Constitution'.[12] The 'Vindication' was written, it is true, for an immediate political object, to defend the House of Lords and, more specifically, the conduct of Disraeli's patron, Lord Lyndhurst, who had led a group of Tory peers attempting to block the legislation of Melbourne's Whig government. Disraeli's initial target was the Benthamite Radicals, or Utilitarians, who seemed to believe that a constitution was something that could be invented by applying abstract principles, and who ignored the fact that the roots of the English Constitution were buried deep in the nation's past. 'With us it has been the growth of ages, and brooding centuries have watched over and tended its perilous birth and feeble infancy. The noble offspring of liberty and law now flourishes in the full and lusty vigor of its proud and perfect manhood.'[13] Disraeli's was a purely Burkean, 'prescriptive' view of the folly of seeking to discard long-established political institutions. The House of Lords, in fact, represented the permanent interests of the nation, and Disraeli extolled the high character of the aristocracy, whose vast territorial property encouraged a sense of social responsibility, public-spiritedness and patriotism.

Disraeli's central thesis was that recent attacks on the House of Lords, and on other venerable institutions like the Church of England, were not isolated incidents but part of a general pattern of aggression from the Utilitarian Radicals and their partners in political crime, the Whigs. Indeed, Disraeli believed that the country was witnessing a repetition of earlier, lamentable periods in its history. He drew a parallel, for instance, between the conduct of the Whigs since coming into office in 1830 and that of their predecessors after the Hanoverian succession of 1714. At both these points in time, Disraeli alleged, the Whigs had carried out 'coups d'état', rigging the political system in order to establish a monopoly of power for themselves. Thus, after 1714 the first two Georges had been the prisoners of the Whigs, more like Venetian Doges than real Kings; and the Whigs had consolidated their hold on the government through systematic corruption and by carrying the Septennial Act (1716), which meant that general elections were only held every seven years instead of every three years. The Whigs, according to Disraeli, had ruled in alliance with two sectional groups, the dissenters and the monied interest of the City of London, but 'The rest of the nation — that is to say, nine-tenths of the people of England — formed the Tory party, the landed proprietors and peasantry of the Kingdom, headed by a spirited and popular Church, and looking to the Kingly power in the abstract, though not to the reigning King, as their only protection from an impending oligarchy.'[14] (Recent research suggests that, while Disraeli was obviously exaggerating, it is true that the Whig regime never commanded majority support in the country as a whole.[15]) Tory ideals had been kept alive, after 1714, by one of Disraeli's great heroes, Lord Bolingbroke, and later on King George III and Pitt the Younger succeeded in breaking the Whigs' oligarchical grip and restoring a truly national Tory government. Unfortunately, the Tories subsequently went into political decline between 1815 and 1830, opening the door for the Whigs to seize power and make another attempt to entrench themselves in office. The Great Reform Act was a piece of electoral gerrymandering, designed to work to the Whigs' own benefit by magnifying the power of their allies, the dissenters. As a result, the Whigs were once more governing in a sectarian spirit: the King had become a political prisoner; institutions like the House of Lords and the Church of England were being menaced; and the Municipal Corporations were under attack, as the Whigs strove to centralise power in their own hands. History was thus being repeated, in Disraeli's view, because:

> the Whigs are an anti-national party. In order to accomplish their object of establishing an oligarchical republic, and of concentrating the government of the State in the hands of a few great families, the Whigs are compelled to declare war against all those great national institutions the power and influence of which make us a nation.

Mercifully, the Tory party could be looked to for salvation because it was 'the national party', indeed 'the really democratic party of England', dedicated to upholding those ancient institutions which alone secured the civil rights of the people.[16]

Disraeli returned to the attack on the Whigs in a series of letters published in *The Times* in the first half of 1836, using the pseudonym 'Runnymede'.[17] The Runnymede letters are characterised by their vituperative onslaught against the Whigs, both individual Ministers and the party as a whole. His comparison of the Whigs with a herd of swine, 'guzzling and grunting in a bed of mire, fouling themselves, and bedaubing every luckless passenger with their contaminating filth' (letter 15), gives some idea of Disraeli's often coarse tone. The Whigs were again indicted as an 'anti-national' party, now becoming increasingly desperate in their attempts to perpetuate their destructive, oligarchic rule. In order to keep themselves in power, they had formed a sordid and dishonest alliance with the group of Irish nationalists led by Daniel O'Connell, whom Disraeli described as the 'hired instrument of the Papacy... a systematic liar and a beggarly cheat, a swindler and a poltroon'; in short, a man motivated by a fundamental hatred of everything English (letters 8 and 16). It is interesting to note, given Disraeli's later policy as Prime Minister in the 1870s, the extent to which he was already emphasising the threat posed to the integrity of the empire by his political opponents (letters 8 and 17). Of more immediate significance was the fulsomeness of Disraeli's tribute to his own leader, Sir Robert Peel, whose 'brief but masterly premiership', in 1834–5, had consolidated the new national party, and in whose 'chivalry...splendid talents and...spotless character' lay the only hope for thwarting the oligarchical Whigs. Disraeli therefore urged Peel to rescue 'our venerable constitution' from the spiteful malignity of Whig rule, and, above all, to 'rescue that mighty body, of which all these great classes and institutions are but some of the constituent and essential parts — rescue THE NATION.' (Letter 5.)

Before Disraeli had entered the House of Commons, then, he had already developed what was to prove a durable conceptual framework for explaining both history and current politics, one which employed the rhetoric of protecting ancient institutions and safeguarding popular liberties, and which stressed the need for government by a 'national' party capable of adapting to changing circumstances. This framework was fundamentally at odds with the 'Whig' interpretation of history, exemplified by the writings of Thomas Babington Macaulay, who detected a linear growth in political liberty, since the 17th century, achieved by *curbing* the powers of those institutions so dear to Disraeli, like the Monarchy. Macaulay's was to become the dominant version of English history by the middle of the 19th century, but in the 1830s Disraeli was still able to propagate a very different view of the past, and in this way to 'vindicate' both the Tory party and his own erratic political course.

Member of Parliament, 1837–41

While Disraeli's election for Maidstone in 1837 obviously marked an important breakthrough, his long-term future in politics remained in considerable doubt. His personal debts had continued to mount up, owing to his extravagant lifestyle and the cost of his various election contests, and he had only been able to stand at Maidstone thanks to the assistance of his colleague in the representation of this two-member borough, Wyndham Lewis, to whom Disraeli was consequently indebted to the tune of about £5,000. In an age when Members of Parliament did not receive a salary, it was hard to see how Disraeli could survive for very long, and he certainly did not have the financial means to fight another general election. Thus, there was a very real prospect that, once deprived of his parliamentary privilege, Disraeli might end up in a debtors' prison.

Disraeli was in desperate need of a stroke of good fortune, and it came in March 1838 when Wyndham Lewis died suddenly. There can be no doubt that Disraeli's marriage, the following year, to Lewis's widow, Mary Anne, was principally motivated by pecuniary considerations, although the marriage turned out to be a success in personal terms as well. Mary Anne had a life interest in her husband's estate — in other words, she received the income from it during her lifetime, but on her death the estate would revert to the Lewis family — which at least provided Disraeli with a financial lifeline, enabling him to pay off some of his more pressing debts and to obtain new credit. Even so, it has been estimated that in 1841 Disraeli's debts were probably in the region of £30,000, which, converted to 1990s money values, would be about £1 million. Without Mary Anne's help in easing the financial pressures on him, Disraeli might very well have gone under. She also gave him the motherly devotion — Mary Anne was twelve years Disraeli's senior — that he so obviously needed from his relationships with women, and it does seem that he became genuinely devoted to her.[18] Furthermore, Disraeli's marriage conferred a degree of social respectability on him which was valuable for political purposes: prior to the 1840 session of Parliament, for instance, the Disraelis hosted a series of political dinners at their Grosvenor Gate residence in London.

The beginning of Disraeli's parliamentary career is always remembered for his disastrous maiden speech, in December

1837, when he was howled down by fractious elements in the House of Commons. This was an unusual incident, for it was normally a matter of parliamentary etiquette to give a maiden speaker a fair hearing. The fact that this courtesy was not extended to Disraeli was partly due to the irritation caused by his flamboyant style of dress, and to the provocative arrogance of a member who had only been in the Commons for a few weeks trying to take the House by storm. But it should also be remembered that much of the commotion emanated from the radicals and the O'Connellites, political groupings with no reason to love Disraeli, and so his hostile reception was in a way a tribute to the reputation he had already made for himself through his writings.

For the remainder of the 1837–41 parliament, Disraeli devoted himself to retrieving his position in the House of Commons, being content to make mostly brief and unspectacular speeches on a wide range of subjects. These more modest efforts seem to have had the desired effect, and some did receive coverage in the press, suggesting that he was making his mark. In Disraeli's own mind, however, each speech was a more complete triumph than the last one, and he believed himself to be establishing a commanding position in the House. His frequent letters to his devoted sister, Sarah, detail this probably largely imaginary advance. On one occasion, in March 1838, he reported that he had made the best speech of the evening, and 'sat down amid loud cheers'. He claimed that he had 'become very popular in the house; I ascribe it to the smoking room.' The following month, Disraeli reckoned he had made 'a most brilliant and triumphant speech...Unquestionably...the crack speech of the night.' Towards the close of the 1839 session, he delivered what he considered to be his finest speech yet and boasted that 'The complete command of the house I now have is remarkable. The moment I rose perfect silence...Members running from the lib[rar]y and all hurrying to their seats.'[19]

It is quite clear that during his early years in parliament Disraeli regarded himself as a loyal follower of Sir Robert Peel. Early in the 1838 session, for instance, he wrote to his leader offering to produce a manifesto of 'the views and principles of the Conservative Party', but this suggestion was politely declined. Disraeli also seems to have made a point of trying to sit behind Sir Robert in the House of Commons.[20] Nevertheless, some of his interventions in debates would not have been at all welcome to his leader, and they show that Disraeli was still capable of taking a highly independent line. On 12 July 1839, when the House was debating whether or not to receive the great petition drawn up by the Chartists, Disraeli expressed his sympathy with the underlying causes of that movement, although he did not agree that universal manhood suffrage was the right solution. From Disraeli's point of view, Chartism was another symptom of the years of misrule by the Whigs and their radical allies, who had failed to protect the rights of the people. One measure that was a particular target for Disraeli's criticism was the new Poor Law of 1834, inspired by the Utilitarian Radicals, which had imposed a dangerous degree of centralisation onto the administration of the system, and, in its quest for economy, had inflicted inhumane treatment on the recipients of poor relief, who were required to submit to the workhouse test. It was little wonder, Disraeli argued, that the people had been persuaded to believe that democratic reform was the only answer to their problems.

Disraeli, then, was able to fit the anti-Poor Law movement in the country, and the Chartist agitation which largely grew out of it, into the analytical framework laid down in his earlier writings such as the 'Vindication of the English Constitution'. The 'anti-national' Whigs were again found guilty of governing in the interests of sectional groups, who in no way represented the feelings and needs of the majority of the people. It was therefore the responsibility of the Conservatives to assert their claim to be the party of the whole nation, including even the unenfranchised masses. There is a fascinating letter from Disraeli to Charles Attwood (the brother of Thomas, founder of the Birmingham Political Union), written in the summer of 1840, in response to Attwood's report of a successful meeting at Newcastle involving local Conservatives and working-class Radicals. This letter suggests that there was a real continuity in Disraeli's political thinking:

> I entirely agree with you, that 'an union between the Conservative party and the Radical Masses' offers the only means by which we can preserve the Empire. Their interests are identical; united they form the Nation; and their division has only permitted a miserable minority, under the specious name of the People, to spoil all rights of property and person.
>
> Since I first entered public life, now eight years ago, I have worked for no other object and no other end, than to aid the formation of a National Party...
>
> None but those devoid of the sense and spirit of Englishmen can be blind to the perils that are impending over our Country. Our empire is assailed in every quarter; while a domestic oligarchy, under the guise of Liberalism, is denationalising England.
>
> Hitherto we have been preserved from the effects of the folly of modern legislation by the wisdom of our ancient manners. The national character may yet save the empire.[21]

Such an alliance between the Conservatives and the masses was not entirely fanciful. At the general election of 1841 Conservatives and Chartists did co-operate in certain constituencies, in common opposition to the Poor Law policy of the Whigs and Radicals.[22]

The problem for Disraeli was that these possibly genuine expressions of social concern were out of step with the views of the Conservative leadership. Peel, for instance, had always supported the Poor Law reform of 1834. While Disraeli may have conceived of himself as a loyal and invaluable member of the Conservative party, the perception of him at the top of the hierarchy was as a troublemaker with strange radical tendencies. Consequently, after the Conservatives' electoral triumph of August 1841 which brought Peel to power at the head of a majority administration, there was no place in it for Disraeli (who had been elected for the borough of Shrewsbury). This was undoubtedly a profound disappointment for Disraeli, who was still badly in need of an official salary, and he expressed his feelings in a well-known letter to Peel:[23] but the brutal truth of the matter is that there is no evidence that he was even considered for office. Disraeli's exclusion from Peel's government in 1841 was, of course, to have serious repercussions in the future, but it may be thought that it was just as well that he was left out. The point is not simply that, if Disraeli had been a minister, he would not have had the freedom to attack Peel's leadership in the way he later did, but also that his political strength never lay in a marked aptitude for administration. Peel, in 1841, included in his government several talented men, such as W. E. Gladstone, Sidney Herbert and Lord Lincoln, all of them Oxford-educated and all of them several years younger than Disraeli, and one wonders whether Disraeli could have climbed very far up the ministerial ladder faced with this sort of competition. It may well be the case, in other words, that Disraeli eventually reached the top in the only way that was feasible for a man of his particular political lineage and skills.

Young England

Disraeli's frustration at being denied a place in Peel's government is evident from a letter to his wife, written early in 1842, in which he complained of feeling 'utterly isolated. Before the change of Government, political party was a tie among men, but now it is only a tie among men who are in office. The supporter of administration, who is not in place & power himself, is a solitary animal. He has neither hope, nor fear.'[24] There were some ominous hints in this of future trouble for Peel, but for the time being Disraeli resisted the temptation to indulge in outright opposition to the government. Indeed, he supported the main planks of Peel's fiscal and commercial policy during the 1842 session. The budget of that year marked the beginning of the Prime Minister's great experiment in Free Trade, involving the wholesale reduction (and in some cases the complete abolition) of tariffs on imports and exports, but this required the reintroduction of the income tax (a controversial step in peacetime) as a 'temporary' device to fill the gap in the government's revenue. Disraeli spoke in support of the income tax, although it is noticeable that he did so on rather different grounds from Peel, arguing that it was unavoidable because of the cost of the Afghan war — an inheritance from Melbourne's government.[25] He had also voted for the reduction in the level of protection provided by the sliding scale on the Corn Laws, in spite of rumours at the time of the division that he was going to join with a small group of Conservative malcontents in opposing Peel's measure. Disraeli's loyalty to the government on this issue, as he observed to his wife, had been 'most *politic and necessary.*'[26]

It was entirely predictable, all the same, that a man of Disraeli's temperament and ambition would be on the lookout for opportunities of making an impression in the House of Commons. In March 1842 he spoke for two hours and twenty minutes on a motion he had introduced calling for the amalgamation of the consular and diplomatic services (Disraeli's target being the conduct of the previous Whig administration). Although he did not force the issue to a division, he made the usual claim afterwards that his 'success was complete & brilliant.' More significant than the motion itself was Disraeli's remark, in the same letter to Mary Anne, that 'all young England, the new members &c, were deeply impressed.' Indeed, two days later he observed that 'I already find myself with[ou]t effort the leader of a party — chiefly of the youth, & new members. Ld. John Manners came to me about a motion which he wanted me to bring forward... Henry Baillie the same about Affghanistan [sic]. I find my position changed.'[27]

Already, it seems, Disraeli was beginning to create a small nucleus of followers, drawn from the younger, idealistic and probably somewhat bored aristocratic members of the Conservative Party,[28] who were eventually to be associated with the name 'Young England'. As his letters to Mary Anne (cited above) suggest, Young England originally meant, as far as Disraeli was concerned, simply that: a party of the Conservative youth, without any specific commitment to a programme of social measures. When it was decided in the autumn of 1842 that the Young Englanders should act together in a concerted way, the initial basis for operations was intended to be a rather bizarre project of Disraeli's for a pro-French foreign policy, which he embodied in a memorandum sent to the King of France, Louis Philippe.[29] Furthermore, some of the most effective attacks made on Peel's government by the Young Englanders, during the 1843 and 1844 sessions, came in the field of Irish policy, where Disraeli displayed a sensitive concern for the plight of the peasantry which was in quite stunning contrast to the vituperative attacks on the character of the Irish people in the 'Runnymede' letters of 1836.[30]

However, it is also true that Young England's criticisms of Peel's government, in 1843–4, focused on certain domestic 'social' issues, notably the working of the Poor Law system and the question of factory hours. With respect to the latter, they supported Lord Ashley's ten-hour amendment to the 1844 Factory Bill. These were the sort of issues that were central to the concerns of the Cambridge-educated aristocratic or landed men, Lord John Manners, George Smythe and Alexander Baillie-Cochrane, all in their twenties, who formed the core of the Young England party, and whose thinking on social questions had evolved quite independently of Disraeli. The essence of Young England ideology lay in its rejection of the rationalist system of thought associated with the political economists and Utilitarian Radicals, which seemed to have infected the minds of governments of both parties during the 1830s and 1840s. Young England was appalled by the 'false' social values of the industrial towns, where human beings were treated as mere commodities and discarded whenever their labour was not required. They looked instead to the re-creation of a stable, hierarchical society, like that of feudal England, in which the reciprocal obligations between rich and poor were acknowledged. It was therefore essential, if a healthy state of social relations was to be restored, to rejuvenate the ancient institutions of the country: the Crown had to be revered again, as a symbol of national unity; the

21

aristocracy had to fulfil its duty by protecting the welfare of the people; and, above all, the Church had to be galvanised into promoting a greater sense of community. Faith and imagination, not reason, were the vital attributes of a society at ease with itself. Of course, it is very easy to scoff at the Young England movement for the way it harked back to a fictitious golden age and for its failure to provide any practical remedies for the problems of the industrial towns, other than more holidays and better recreational facilities. But it must be remembered that Young England was by no means unique in its fascination with the country's medieval past. On the contrary, there was a powerful cult of medievalism in the early decades of the 19th century, which manifested itself in a wide variety of the forms: the Oxford Movement in religion; the Gothic Revival in architecture (also, a little later, the Pre-Raphaelite Movement in art); the novels of Sir Walter Scott; the political, historical and philosophical writings of Hallam, Coleridge and Carlyle, along with many other works, were all inspired by a sense of the importance of recovering those 'true' social values that had been lost sight of in the conditions of the modern world.[31]

Disraeli's great contribution to Young England came through his two most famous novels, *Coningsby or The New Generation* (1844), and *Sybil, or the Two Nations* (1845). The eponymous hero of *Coningsby* is a young aristocrat searching for a meaning in politics, in an age of expediency, by restoring true Tory principles to his party (an obvious hit at Peel's leadership), while *Sybil* is notable for its attempt to provide an authentic portrayal of the life of the poor in the industrial towns, drawing heavily on the evidence published in official reports. Perhaps the most interesting point about these novels, from a historian's perspective, is that they rest upon an interpretation of history which has been considerably revised since Disraeli's writings of the mid-1830s, like the 'Vindication of the English Constitution'.[32] Whereas in the 'Vindication' we were told that the Venetian oligarchy imposed by the Whigs in 1714 was broken by George III and Pitt the Younger, it turns out instead, according to *Coningsby*, that George and Pitt had failed in their attempt to rid themselves of the Whigs' republican system and that 'a Venetian Constitution did govern England from the accession of the House of Hanover until 1832.' (Bk. V, Ch. 2.) This enabled Disraeli to launch into his celebrated condemnation of those 'pseudo-Tories' responsible for governing the country between 1815 and 1830, including the unfortunate Lord Liverpool, the 'Arch-Mediocrity', whose obstinate resistance to all reform had prevented the Tory party from broadening its public appeal. (Bk. II, Ch. 1.) In the 'Vindication', on the other hand, Disraeli's comments about Liverpool and his colleagues had been very mild, their only fault apparently being that they were *too* reformist! Similarly, whereas the Disraeli of the mid-1830s had hailed Peel as the saviour of the country, by the mid-1840s the moderate, reformist 'Conservatism' embodied in Peel's Tamworth Manifesto (1834) had become 'an attempt to construct a party without principles.' Peel's brand of Conservatism was now denounced for its failure to assert the rights of ancient institutions, like the Crown, the Church and the House of Lords, which were conserved only so long as they did not exercise their powers. It appeared that Peel was content merely to seek political compromises with the enemies of these institutions, in order to secure temporary lulls in radical agitation. Disraeli's verdict, therefore, was that Conservatism 'offers no redress for the Present, and makes no preparation for the Future.' (Bk. II, Ch. 5.)

There is no way of telling whether the revisions in Disraeli's interpretation of history were carried out consciously or unconsciously, but it is clear that what he had done was to adapt his earlier conceptual framework so as to incorporate into it both the political fact of his increasing alienation from Peel's leadership and his more recent Young England concerns. This latter point can be illustrated by reference to *Sybil*, where a social dimension is added to Disraeli's account of English history almost entirely absent from works like the 'Vindication'. In *Sybil* we are treated to a rosy description of England in medieval times, where it seems that the people lived in comfort, cared for by the Church, which provided hospitals and schools, and by the monasteries, who were gentle landlords.[33] There was also a prosperous class of yeoman farmers. Everything changed, though, after the dissolution of the monasteries in the 16th century, and there was no longer a sense of community in England: the way had been opened, in fact, for the growth of cities and the cult of individualism, which set men in competition against one another and made them careless of their neighbours. (Bk. II, ch. 5.) And who had been the beneficiaries of the dissolution of the monasteries? The answer, of course, was a new class of rapacious plunderers who formed the basis for the Whig aristocracy, and who subsequently gained a political stranglehold over the country by undermining its ancient institutions. (Bk. I, Ch. 3.)

As far as practical remedies for England's current malaise were concerned, Disraeli looked above all to the regeneration of the monarchy, which alone could provide an imaginative bond of union. A free monarch ruling an educated people was the vision of the future expressed by Disraeli, through the mouthpiece of his fictional hero, Coningsby: 'a polity capable of great ends and appealing to high sentiments; a polity which, in my opinion, would render government an object of national affection, which would terminate sectional anomalies, assuage religious heats, and extinguish Chartism.' (*Coningsby*, Bk. VII, Ch. 2.) Peel, according to Disraeli, had had a splendid opportunity to 'restore the exercise of that regal authority, the usurpation of whose functions has entailed on the people of England so much suffering and so much degradation', but, regrettably, he had declined the Premiership in 1839 because of a silly squabble over the ladies of the bedchamber, and allowed the Whigs to return to office. Peel had failed to realise that, in the prevailing state of public opinion, 'a movement in favour of prerogative was at hand. The leader of the Tory party should have vindicated his natural position...But we forget, Sir Robert Peel is not the leader of the Tory party.' (*Sybil*, Bk. IV, Ch. 14.)

It would be naïve to suppose that Disraeli's attachment to Young England and its ideals was not primarily motivated by his need for a vehicle with which to publicise himself and, with luck, to further his political career. There are signs as early as the autumn of 1844, after he had made some speeches in the north of England, that Disraeli was inclined to think that Young England, as a political party, had been taken as far as it could go. In a letter to Lord John Manners he agreed that the best thing to be done for the time being was to lie low: 'We have carried to a happy conclusion a highly successful campaign, unquestionably raised our names in the country, ascertained that the feeling of the nation is with us, & having supplied the world with sufficient suggestions, the wisest thing we can do is to leave them to chew the cud.'[34] But the reality, as the 1845 session of parliament showed, was that Young England was virtually moribund. Its ideas may have struck a temporary chord in the country, at a time when it was fashionable to agonise over the 'condition of England', but the conditions described in *Sybil* were those of 1842, when the economy was in the depths of an unusually severe depression, and the situation had improved considerably since then. The Free Trade elixir seemed to have done the trick, and it is interesting to note that in the final chapter of *Sybil*, which appeared in the spring of 1845, the trade on the Mowbray estate has been 'entirely revived' thanks to the 'great measures of Sir Robert Peel.' The dilemma for Disraeli was that he was now forty years of age and, despite all the publicity he had attracted, as far away as ever from securing a place in the Conservative party hierarchy.

The destruction of Sir Robert Peel

However, new tensions in the always difficult relationship between Peel and the Conservative party were about to create opportunities for Disraeli to establish a prominent position in the House of Commons by identifying himself with important sections of backbench opinion. Disraeli had already burned his boats with the leadership when, in June 1844, he launched a direct personal attack on the Prime Minister, accusing him of being a dictator after Peel had compelled Conservative backbenchers to rescind a vote given against his sugar duties policy.[35] During the 1845 session, Peel caused a far greater sense of outrage amongst his own MPs when he proposed to increase and make permanent the State grant to the Roman Catholic seminary at Maynooth. From Peel's point of view, this was a statesmanlike attempt to defuse Irish nationalism by securing the support of the Catholic Church, but to many Conservative MPs it was an affront to the 'Protestant' values which they believed should guide the conduct of the British State. Disraeli seized the chance offered by the Maynooth issue, delivering one of his most remarkable speeches in the Commons, on 11 April, in which he denounced the character of a minister who had demonstrated a lamentable absence of commitment to fixed principles of policy:

> What have we got instead? Something has risen up in this Country as fatal in the political world, as it has been in the landed world of Ireland — we have a great Parliamentary middleman. It is well known what a middleman is; he is a man who bamboozles his own party and plunders the other, till, having obtained a position to which he is not entitled, he cries out 'Let us have no party questions, but fixity of tenure.' I want to have a commission issued to inquire into the tenure by which Downing Street is held...[36]

Curiously, Disraeli's criticism of the Maynooth grant was not directed at the policy itself but against the immorality of the leader of the Conservative party, a body supposedly committed to Protestant principles, implementing such a measure. In fact, Disraeli's stance on this issue was made somewhat awkward by his speeches of 1843–4, sympathising with the Irish people (his two closest Young England friends, Smythe and Manners, actually supported the grant). As it was, Disraeli was just about able to find political ground on which to attack Peel over Maynooth, and in this way to make himself the mouthpiece for backbench Conservatives who felt betrayed by their own leader. The Maynooth grant was finally carried, with the help of Lord John Russell and the Opposition, but one-half of Conservative MPs voted against it.

It was mentioned earlier that Disraeli had been careful to support Peel's Free Trade measures in 1842, and he even went so far as to claim, in a letter to a newspaper editor the following year, that Free Trade was simply a 'recurrence to old Tory principles', a policy in the best traditions of Bolingbroke and Pitt.[37] In 1846, however, an opportunity arose for Disraeli to align himself with the most powerful Conservative element of all, the agricultural interest, when Peel disclosed that it was his intention to apply the principle of Free Trade to the land by repealing the protective tariffs known as the Corn Laws. To the average, inarticulate Conservative country gentleman, Peel's conduct represented a gross betrayal of his party, being quite inconsistent with the declarations made by most Conservative candidates in 1841. Disraeli's role during the crisis of 1846 was to act as the spokesman for the outraged country gentlemen by making a series of devastating attacks on Peel during the lengthy debates on Corn Law repeal.[38] He denounced Peel's attempt to appease hostile middle-class groups like the Anti-Corn Law League by abandoning the interests of landed society. Repeal was presented as a pernicious measure which threatened to undermine the 'territorial constitution', and with it the only guarantee for popular liberties. Disraeli also returned to his personal theme, accusing Peel of being an intellectual lightweight whose ideas were borrowed from others — in other words, his opponents: 'His life has been a great appropriation clause. He is a burglar of others' intellect... there is no Statesman who has committed political petty larceny on so great a scale.' What made Disraeli's onslaught so effective was his tone of mockery — he provoked much laughter on both sides of the House — a form of attack to which the Prime Minister was temperamentally ill-equipped to respond. Disraeli was able to do far more damage to Peel by ridiculing him than he could ever have achieved if he had trespassed onto the Premier's home territory and tried to recite official statistics.[39]

Peel had probably underestimated the intensity of the hostility which his decision to drop protectionism would provoke on the Conservative backbenches and in the constituencies. Agricultural protection societies were active in many areas, and their pressure undoubtedly helped to make the opposition to Peel in the House of Commons more solid than it would otherwise have been. In the House, steps were taken to co-ordinate the efforts of the dissident Conservatives, as Disraeli reported to a Scottish correspondent in March 1846: 'Here we are involved in a struggle of ceaseless excitement & energy. Deserted by our leaders, even by the subalterns of the camp, we have been obliged to organise ourselves, & choose chieftains from the rank & file'.[40] The great handicap under which the protectionist Conservatives laboured, as Disraeli's letter indicates, was the fact that virtually the whole of the front bench supported Peel's initiative, the only leader of real consequence to oppose him being Lord Stanley, who sat in the Upper House. It was due to these unique circumstances that Disraeli was able to push himself forward into a prominent position, as there was a chronic shortage of debating talent within the protectionist ranks. Disraeli certainly made himself indispensable to his party, but it is important to remember that, at this stage, he would have been considered quite unacceptable as a leader of the Conservative country gentlemen. This role was filled by a hitherto obscure MP, Lord George Bentinck, whose high social status (he was the son of a Duke) and obvious honesty of purpose meant that he could command the respect and loyalty of the country gentlemen, in spite of his limitations as a debater.

The 222 protectionist Conservatives who voted against the third reading of the Corn Law Repeal Bill on 15 May were not in the end strong enough to stop Peel, because the votes of the Prime Minister and his 120 Conservative supporters were supplemented by those of Russell and the Opposition. Subsequently, the influence of the Duke of Wellington was decisive in persuading the House of Lords to pass the bill. However, another issue was available on which Peel was vulnerable to attack: his proposed Irish Arms Bill. On this question, the Opposition was resolved to vote against the government, and this made it possible for the protectionists to force Peel's resignation by helping to defeat the measure. Conservative MPs were normally very much in favour of coercing the Irish, and it is a good indication of the depth of their bitterness towards Peel that 69 of them were prepared to vote against the Arms Bill, thereby denying Peel any chance of soldiering on in office and perhaps finding some means of reuniting his party. At the Carlton Club, when the news of Peel's resignation was announced, Disraeli wrote triumphantly to his wife: 'All "Coningsby & Young England" the general exclamation here.'[41] Yet it was hardly that, for of Disraeli's closest Young England associates only Manners opposed the repeal of the Corn Laws, whereas Baillie-Cochrane supported Peel's government and Smythe had actually agreed to join it.

Disraeli and the Conservative Party

Throughout his career, doubts were frequently expressed about the sincerity of Disraeli's political convictions. Radicals, in the early 1830s, had questioned whether he was really one of them; Peel, later in the decade, was evidently unimpressed by Disraeli's attempt at being a Conservative loyalist; Lord John Manners, personally devoted though he was to Disraeli, wondered whether he really believed in the principles of Young England;[42] and, in 1846, it must have astonished many observers to see Disraeli setting himself up as the spokesman of the country gentlemen. It is easy to say that he was just an opportunist, but we should not neglect the power of Disraeli's imagination, his ability to project himself into the mind-set of those whose cause he happened to be espousing. And it is important to remember that, in all his political manifestations, Disraeli was not merely an adherent but a *publiciser*, invariably succeeding in justifying his views by reference to a bold interpretation of English history.

The value of imagination in politics is a recurring theme in Disraeli's thought. In his 'mutilated diary' entry for 1833, we find his growing dislike of Benthamite Radicalism expressed in the revealing declaration that 'The Utilitarians in Politics are like the Unitarians in religion. Both omit Imagination in their systems, and Imagination governs mankind.' Likewise, more than a decade later, the ultimate, damning judgement he could make about Peel was that he was 'with[ou]t imagination or any inspiring qualities.'[43] Disraeli in fact never repudiated his early views and, as late as 1870, in the general preface to a new edition of his complete novels, he explained that the Young England trilogy, contrary to the dominant Utilitarian spirit of the time, had 'recognised imagination in the government of nations as a quality not less important than reason.'[44] It was surely the potential inherent in the monarchy, as an instrument for cultivating feelings of reverence and loyalty among the masses, which so attracted Disraeli during his Young England phase, rather than any belief in the practical possibility of restoring the Crown to its earlier position of political supremacy.

At the same time, imagination offered a means by which a social outsider, a man from a literary, middle-class background, of Jewish origins and foreign appearance, could integrate himself into a political culture dominated by the aristocratic and landed elite. Professor Paul Smith has argued, in a stimulating paper, that Disraeli's politics should be seen as 'the politics of denizenation, of settlement, the means by which Disraeli could achieve a sense of home'.[45] Through his writings, from the 'Vindication' to the Young England novels, Disraeli evolved an idiosyncratic view of English history which permitted him to create a suitable political vehicle out of the Conservative party. By claiming a unique insight both into the national past — in the final chapter of *Sybil* he maintained that the Whig oligarchy had successfully blotted out from people's minds the *real* history of the past ten reigns — as well as into its future destiny, Disraeli was effectively asserting his right to be the leader of the people, rather like a magus or wise man. It did not matter that he conveniently changed the details of his historical interpretation over the years so that they accorded with developing political circumstances. Even Disraeli's Jewishness did not pose such a problem for him as might have been expected, for he was able to construct an imaginative identity for himself as an aristocrat, based on his beliefs about his particular Jewish ancestry. The Disraeli family were Sephardic Jews, the branch which he considered to be aristocratic (as opposed to the Ashkenazim), and he also invented a romantic past for his family as the descendants of Jews expelled from Spain in 1492.[46] Furthermore, Disraeli managed to reconcile his Jewish past with his conversion to Anglicanism by asserting, most famously in the final novel in his Young England trilogy, *Tancred or the New Crusade*, (published in 1847), that Christianity, after all, was nothing more than completed Judaism. Such self-perceptions explain why he found remarkably little difficulty in moving in the highest social circles: unlike, say, W. E. Gladstone, the Oxford-educated son of a Liverpool merchant, Disraeli was never regarded as an awkward parvenu. The Conservative party did not realise it in 1846, but it had found a man who considered himself fitted by destiny to be its leader.

2

THE MID-VICTORIAN CONSERVATIVE PARTY

Introduction

The Corn Law crisis of 1846 and the downfall of Sir Robert Peel inaugurated a long period in which the Liberals held a virtual monopoly of government in Great Britain. Between 1846 and 1865 the Conservatives were only briefly in office on two occasions, from February to December 1852, and February 1858 to June 1859, and both of these involved minority administrations which existed solely because of temporary divisions on the Liberal side. Stanley, Bentinck and Disraeli, by inspiring the Conservative rebellion against Peel, had in effect incited their party to press the political self-destruct button, and it was to take decades before the damage was repaired. The fundamental difficulty for the Conservatives was that in repudiating Peel they had deprived themselves of the assistance of almost every other member of their front bench, and although Peel himself was never to hold office again — he died as a result of a riding accident in 1850 — his most talented and influential followers were to gravitate towards the Liberals in the course of the 1850s. This loss of ministerial expertise meant that the Conservatives suffered from a serious credibility problem, which was not helped by the fact that their policy of restoring agricultural protection became so discredited that by 1852 the party had abandoned it. If the Conservatives' predicament did not seem entirely hopeless at the time, it was because relations between the Liberals and the 'Peelites' were tempestuous and slow to mature, and because the Liberals themselves — an incongruous mix of Whigs, Radicals and independent Irish MPs — were prone to internal conflict. Liberal divisions did indeed provide the Conservatives with a few political opportunities, but in the event they proved unable to capitalise on them, and after June 1859, when Lord Palmerston succeeded in forming a more integrated Liberal government (including the surviving Peelites) the Conservatives found that they could do little against him: they were left waiting for his death in the hope that this might create a more favourable situation.

Disraeli and the Conservative leadership, 1846–52

Lord Stanley, who succeeded his father as the 14th Earl of Derby in 1851, was the unquestioned leader of the Conservative party throughout the period covered in this chapter, but as he sat in the upper House he needed to have an efficient lieutenant to take responsibility for leading the party in the House of Commons. This role was eventually to be filled by Disraeli, although he had to surmount a formidable barrier of social prejudice and political suspicion, and not everyone was entirely reconciled to his leadership. In the aftermath of the Corn Law crisis, Disraeli had been able to gradually build upon the position which he had made for himself through his attacks on Peel. For instance, he found that he now enjoyed a certain degree of social respectability, and the doors of some of the greatest stately homes, like Belvoir Castle and Burghley House, were opened to him. He was able to further consolidate his status through the acquisition of a modest country house and estate, Hughenden Manor in Buckinghamshire: the patrimony received on the death of his father provided some of the financial wherewithal, but Disraeli could never have purchased the property without a loan of £25,000 from members of the Bentinck family. Hughenden was important to Disraeli, not merely as a pleasant rural retreat but for the standing it gave him within the county, which enabled him to secure election as one of the members for Buckinghamshire at the general election in the summer of 1847.[1] Disraeli thus became a 'knight of the shire', in parliamentary terms, a dignity that was virtually a prerequisite for anyone seeking to lead the party of the landed interest. Characteristically, in his address to the electors of Buckinghamshire, Disraeli assured them that he had always 'upheld the cause of the Territorial Constitution of England, as the best and surest foundation for popular rights and public liberty, imperial power and social happiness.' It followed that 'The maintenance of the agricultural industry of the country is the necessary condition of the enjoyment of that Constitution.'[2]

Subsequent events helped to catapult Disraeli into a position of authority which he could never have expected to achieve so quickly, if at all. During the 1847 session of Parliament Lord George Bentinck acted as Conservative leader in the lower House, but at the end of the year he resigned following criticism of his support for the cause of Jewish emancipation. Bentinck had never been temperamentally suited to the task of leadership and, in some ways, despite his ferocious attacks on Peel for betraying the landed interest, he was perhaps rather too 'liberal' for his party (as a 'Canningite', in the 1820s, he had favoured Catholic emancipation, and he later supported the Great Reform Bill).[3] More curious still is the fact that Disraeli also voted for the admission of Jews into Parliament, and yet he was not subjected to the same censure as Bentinck: presumably it had been expected from someone often contemptuously referred to, by backbench Conservatives, as 'the Jew'. In February 1848 Lord Granby, the elder brother of Disraeli's close friend, Lord John Manners, agreed to assume the leadership, but he resigned after only a month, frankly admitting that he lacked the necessary personal qualities for the post. For the remainder of the session, the Conservatives were without an official leader in the House of Commons, although Stanley did his best to manage matters through the agency of the party whips, Beresford and Newdegate, who were his creatures. A significant breakthrough for Disraeli, in terms of political recognition, came at the close of the session, when Stanley asked him to make a general speech surveying the failings of the Liberal government. Disraeli, for one, was delighted with his oratorical performance and the publicity it attracted, telling his sister afterwards: 'The success is universal. I never knew a greater parliamentary *coup*. The County papers teem with articles...Such is life.'[4]

Just a few weeks later, the political situation was transformed by the sudden death of Bentinck, at the age of only 46. Bentinck had remained active during the 1848 session, encouraging the hope that he might be induced to resume the Conservative leadership, but with his departure from the scene the field was left very much open for Disraeli. However, Stanley was still wary of Disraeli, and prior to the 1849 session he tried to persuade him to defer to the veteran frontbencher, J. C. Herries. This proposed arrangement was torpedoed by Disraeli, who replied to Stanley indicating that he might be driven to adopt an independent position: 'in the present distracted state of parties, it is my opinion... that I co[ul]d do more to uphold the cause to wh. I am attached, that I should have better opportunities of reviving the spirit, & raising the general tone of feeling among our friends throughout the Country, by acting alone & unshackled, than if I fell into the party discipline wh. you intimate.'[5] There was an implicit threat in this letter that Disraeli might well cause trouble from the backbenches if an unacceptable leader was imposed over his head. He busied himself in the meantime in rallying as much support as he could from those Conservative peers and MPs who regarded his services as indispensable to the party, and who were prepared to advise Stanley accordingly.[6] Under considerable pressure, Stanley suggested a compromise solution involving a joint leadership between Granby, Herries and Disraeli. In fact, Disraeli never formally agreed to this 'triumvirate' either, but after a meeting with Stanley, at the end of January, he decided to tacitly go along with it, confident that his superior debating skills would mark him out as the real leader, and that he would gradually be able to overcome the suspicion and distrust felt towards him by many Conservative backbenchers.[7]

Disraeli's not unreasonable fear during the leadership crisis of January 1849 was that the Conservative party wanted to make use of his debating powers for the moment, while being ready to discard or relegate him if and when the political situation improved. In a revealing letter to Prince Metternich, the former Austrian Chancellor now living in exile in England, Disraeli acknowledged that it was certainly 'a great anomaly, that a proud aristocracy should find a chief in one, who is not only not an aristocrat, but against whose origin exist other prejudices, than being merely a man of the people' (he was referring to his Jewish background). But he believed that 'the irresistible force of circumstances' was about to place him in a leading position:

> My own feeling is briefly this. I am prepared to follow any leader, whom my party may elect, provided always that the leader is able to lead. I will not undertake the burthen of debate in a subordinate position, because the inevitable & humiliating inference from such conduct on my part would be, that I was a man fit to be used, but not to be trusted.

> The very fact that I am not an aristocrat renders it, to my mind, still more necessary, that my position shd be assured, & my character enforced & sustained; to increase my influence in a struggle where I have, at the same time, to watch the Whigs, check Sir Robert Peel, & beat back the revolutionary waves of the Manchester School [i.e. Radicals].[8]

While Disraeli may fairly be described as the *de facto* leader of the Conservatives in the House of Commons from 1849 onwards, the wider political context remained as complicated and confused as it had ever been since the Corn Law crisis. When Peel resigned as Prime Minister in June 1846, Lord John Russell had formed a Liberal government committed to maintaining Free Trade, but his hold on office frequently appeared tenuous because he could never rely on the support of Radicals and independent Irish Liberals on the backbenches. The only reason why Russell's Ministry survived as long as it did was that neither the Peelites nor the Conservatives were anxious to destroy it. Peel himself was not prepared to bring down the Liberals if the likely result was to be the formation of a Stanley administration dedicated to restoring protectionism, and he was therefore ready to come to Russell's rescue whenever the government was in jeopardy. From the Conservatives' point of view, on the other hand, the great danger was that if Russell's government fell it might lead to the creation of a Liberal-Peelite coalition, thus destroying any hope of a Conservative-Peelite reunion. As Disraeli had put it in a letter to a foreign correspondent in August 1846, 'We have no wish to defeat them [the Liberals]. It will require some time before our party is re-organised on a comprehensive basis.' He even speculated on the possibility that Gladstone, one of the prominent younger Peelites, might offer himself as 'the future leader of the Tory party', rallying everyone under his banner and 'leaving Peel stranded.'[9] No doubt this particular idea was fanciful, but the essential point remains that, for some years after 1846, a Conservative-Peelite reconciliation seemed to be on the cards, if only their self-inflicted wounds could be allowed to heal quietly.

Indeed, some of the rank-and-file Peelite MPs did drift back to the main Conservative body over the next few years.[10] This reflected the fact that the group of 85 or 90 MPs nominally reckoned to be Peelites after the 1847 general election did not function as a regular, organised party, since Peel rejected the idea that he should act as a party leader. Consequently, there was an exceptionally fluid situation on the backbenches, in the House of Commons, with many of the supposed Peelites, and also a good number of the 225–30 Conservative MPs, lacking any fixed allegiance to either Stanley or Peel and preferring to wait and see how matters developed. In these delicate circumstances, Disraeli and other parliamentary leaders needed to be tactically adroit. For instance, he explained to one correspondent why the Conservatives had not moved a vote of no confidence against Russell's government at the start of the 1848 session: 'I calculate that the Government might have had 200 majority — all the Peelites & trimmers being then prepared to support them.'[11] Two years later, on the other hand, Disraeli scored a significant triumph when he introduced resolutions on the subject of agricultural distress which, by carefully omitting any mention of protectionism, attracted much Conservative and Peelite support. According to the young Edward Stanley, son of the Conservative leader, Disraeli's resolutions 'fell like a shell in the Peelite camp, and for a time completely divided that party. All who wished to stand well with both sides, and looked forward to a future reconciliation, voted with us.'[12]

With regard to the Peelite *leaders*, however, the problem remained, as Disraeli observed in September 1846, that 'the conservative rancour flourishes in all its primal virulence & vigor.' [13] Feelings were so strong on the Conservative back-benches, and among the agriculturalists in the constituencies, that reunion with the 'treacherous' Peelites was not likely to be easily achieved. In fact, the agricultural depression of the late 1840s, caused by bad harvests and plentiful supplies of cheap imported cereals, only served to make the landed interest more intransigent in its demand for a return to protectionist policies.[14] Thus, when Russell's fragile Ministry collapsed through internal weakness in February 1851, Lord Stanley's bid to construct a comprehensive Conservative alternative came to grief because the Peelites, Lord Aberdeen, Lord Canning, and Gladstone (Peel was now dead), declined his offers of Cabinet posts on the grounds that he was still committed to introducing a small fixed duty on corn. To Disraeli's dismay, Stanley abandoned his attempt at ministry-making, and the Queen invited Russell and his colleagues to return to office.[15]

Protectionism, therefore, remained the major obstacle to a Conservative-Peelite rapprochement in the early 1850s. Another issue which emerged at this time served to reinforce the barrier between the two groups: this was the no-popery cry, provoked by Pius IX's decision to re-establish a Roman Catholic hierarchy in England. The Conservatives' instinctive 'Protestant' feelings were outraged by this 'papal aggression', and they readily exploited the opportunity to agitate on the issue in the constituencies. An important feature of this agitation, moreover, was the attack on Anglican High Churchmen who were suspected of being Catholic infiltrators. Since many of the leading Peelites, including Gladstone and Sidney Herbert, were themselves High Churchmen, this inevitably created political ill-feeling and rendered the prospects for an early reconciliation with the Conservative Party unlikely. The only consolation was that Russell's attempt to harness anti-Catholic feeling in the Country, by passing the Ecclesiastical Titles Act in 1851, made a Liberal-Peelite junction equally problematic.

Serious policy differences between the Conservatives and Peelites undoubtedly existed, but the personal dimension was no less important. As Stanley had recognised, in January 1849, there was one individual in particular on the Conservative side who was 'the most powerful *repellent* we could offer to any repentant or hesitating Peelites.'[16] He was referring, of course, to Disraeli, whose personal attacks on Peel in 1846 had not been forgiven by the great man's followers, and this helps to explain Stanley's reluctance to have him as the acknowledged Conservative leader in the House of Commons. The intriguing question therefore arises: did Disraeli really want to see a Conservative-Peelite reunion take place, if it was going to involve some sacrifice of his hard-won position? It is easy to imagine, after all, that while Disraeli might have looked forward to the restoration of a 'comprehensive' Conservative party in 1846, when he was only one of the leading figures on the frontbench and his personal expectations were accordingly limited, by the time he had emerged as *the* leading Conservative in the Commons he might well have been more ambivalent towards a reunion which, although obviously a good thing for the party, would not have been so good for himself.

On the face of things, to be fair to Disraeli, he appears to have acted generously, offering to relinquish the Commons' lead in Gladstone's favour during the abortive negotiations to form a Stanley ministry in February 1851. But many observers at the time thought that Gladstone's uncomfortably intense and overbearing manner prevented him from being an acceptable leader to the Conservative rank-and-file,[17] and so the possibility remains that Disraeli made his offer to give way in the expectation that he would not be required to carry it out. Lord Blake, in his classic biography of Disraeli, has suggested that on an earlier occasion, when the Conservatives and Peelites combined to attack Lord Palmerston's foreign policy (the famous Don Pacifico debate of May 1850), Disraeli may have deliberately pulled his punches for fear that, if the government fell, a Conservative-Peelite administration would take its place.[18] The evidence on this point is inconclusive: Disraeli himself privately maintained that the real danger for the Conservatives lay in the possibility that Palmerston might be forced to resign, enabling the Peelites to join Russell's government; but it is true that Stanley and others were anticipating a Conservative-Peelite reunion as the outcome of the crisis.[19]

Disraeli's true feelings about the prospective return of the Peelites may never be known for certain, but we need to bear in mind that another political option was available. In a letter to Lord John Manners in September 1846, Disraeli had expressed the view that 'ultimately, there must be a fusion bet[wee]n the real Whigs & us.'[20] By the term 'real Whigs', Disraeli meant those aristocratic Liberals who were uneasy with Russell's Premiership, fearing that he was likely to be forced into adopting dangerously radical policies. The key figure, from Disraeli's point of view, was the Foreign Secretary, Palmerston, who was successfully cultivating an image as a populist politician through his 'gunboat diplomacy' and chauvinistic posturing against the European autocracies. Palmerston was known to be at odds with the Prime Minister, partly because of his controversial manner of conducting foreign policy, but also because he was hostile to Russell's wish for a further instalment of parliamentary reform. There was thus a very real prospect of the Conservatives landing a prize catch, if Palmerston could be induced to change sides, which might well serve as a catalyst for further Whig defections from the Liberal party. Disraeli's strategy, in the meantime, was to avoid unnecessary attacks on the Foreign Secretary, a point on which he gave private assurances to a sympathetic Whig peer: 'As for Palmerston, I have not only not opposed him, but, to the occasional dissatisfaction of my comrades, have even interfered to prevent parliamentary criticism, or any concerted move, against him.'[21]

Conservative hopes were naturally raised when in December 1851 Russell finally dismissed his Foreign Secretary, provoking Palmerston to retaliate two months later by voting with the Opposition to defeat the Militia Bill and bring down the government. Stanley (now the Earl of Derby) was invited to form a ministry, and Disraeli made a similar offer to that of the year before, except that he was now proposing to waive his claim to the Commons' leadership in favour of Palmerston. We cannot be sure that Disraeli's offer was sincere, but there was no great obstacle to Palmerston's acceptance of the lead now that he was a political freelance, and such an arrangement would have made a great deal of sense both for the Conservative party, which needed strengthening, and for Disraeli, who could afford to defer to a man twenty years his senior, on the assumption that Palmerston would not remain leader for very long. (No-one could have guessed, of course, that Palmerston would survive until 1865, when he was over 80!) In the event, Palmerston was too cautious to be willing to commit himself to the Conservatives at this stage, but Disraeli continued to believe in the months that followed that he would eventually see his future as lying with the Conservatives, and that he might perhaps bring over with him some leading Peelites like Gladstone and Herbert.[22] In the meantime Derby went ahead and formed a purely Conservative administration, with Disraeli as Chancellor of the Exchequer and Leader of the House of Commons, which, owing to its chronic shortage of ministerial experience, acquired the unhappy nickname of the 'Who? Who? ministry'.

It may well be that, in the period up to 1852, Disraeli ultimately owed his survival as Conservative leader in the lower House to the fact that his party's obstinate adherence to agricultural protectionism barred the way to any political realignment. And yet, ironically, it was Disraeli, more than anyone else, who had been anxious for some time to break the Conservatives' addiction to tariffs, in the belief that this was the only way of broadening the party's appeal. No doubt Disraeli's willingness to jettison protection betrayed the fundamentally opportunistic nature of his attachment to the agriculturalists' cause in 1846, which had always been based far more on the condemnation of Peel's treachery to his party than on any defence of the Corn Laws *per se*. Even in his 1847 election address, Disraeli had stated that the new Free Trade system should be given a fair trial, an early indication that he did not consider it practicable to return to protectionist policies. The death of Bentinck in September 1848 removed what would otherwise have been an insurmountable personal obstacle to a change of political tack on Disraeli's part. Late in 1849, and through much of 1850, he was therefore working out ideas for alternative measures to provide some relief for the agricultural interest, such as transferring part of the burden of local rates on to the Treasury, in order to soften the blow when the Conservative party finally abandoned protectionism. 'The great point', as he explained to Manners, was 'to devise a scheme, wh. will rally the landed party, & yet be suited to the spirit of the age. As for Protection in its old form, I look upon that as dead.'[23] However, the depth of feeling in the Conservatives' county strongholds ruled out any decisive step at this stage, and when Disraeli became Chancellor of the Exchequer in February 1852 the party's position on tariffs was still ambiguous.

Coming into office in February, only weeks before the budget statement was due, Disraeli agreed with the Opposition that he should make interim financial arrangements in April and produce a considered measure later in the year. This gave the Conservatives time to fight a general election in the summer, which brought them a gain of some twenty seats, increasing their total strength to around 300. The victims of the 1852 general election were the Peelites, of whom no more than about forty were returned to the new House of Commons. Nevertheless, the fact that the Conservatives had failed to gain an overall majority released the party leaders, at last, from any remaining sense of obligation to attempt to restore protective tariffs. Disraeli was therefore left with the task of devising a budget which would give some other form of relief to agriculture, without offending against the canons of the new Free Trade orthodoxy. He was evidently determined to introduce a bold measure of financial reorganisation in the hope of seizing the political initiative and improving the government's chances of survival. It is quite possible, as one writer has recently suggested, that Disraeli's object was to appeal to a broad range of 'moderate' opinion:[24] he was still looking, after all, to win over Palmerston and other 'Whigs'. Unfortunately for him, his room for financial manoeuvre was restricted, at a very late stage, by additional demands for defence expenditure. When he made his Budget statement on 3 December he was able to announce reductions in the duties on malt (to please the farmers) and tea, both of which could be presented as fresh instalments of Free Trade, but in order to compensate for the loss in government revenue he proposed a substantial increase in the house tax. This predictably led to complaints that Disraeli was taking money from the pockets of townspeople and transferring it to his friends, the farmers. More serious still, from the point of view of fiscal purists like Gladstone, was Disraeli's plan to introduce an element of differentiation into the income tax, so that those relying on 'precarious' (i.e. earned) incomes would pay at a lower rate than those with 'realised' (unearned) incomes. The great objection to this was that in Peel's original financial scheme of 1842 the income tax had been intended as a temporary expedient, and Gladstone and others were therefore unwilling to countenance a more sophisticated form of income tax assessment, as it implied that the tax was going to be retained for the foreseeable future.[25]

In the early hours of 17 December the Budget was defeated by 305 votes to 286 and Derby's government was obliged to resign. The final night of the debate had been notable for the clash between Disraeli and Gladstone — the beginning of their long political rivalry — accompanied, appropriately enough, by the sound of a violent thunderstorm outside. E. M. Whitty, a journalist, provided the following description of the scene: 'it was the most superb parliamentary duel I ever witnessed.... it was a real debate, in which speech *did* affect votes, and in which each orator was exhausting his powers to obtain a majority.... such a scene could only result from the presence of two such master minds.' Disraeli had risen to deliver his summing-up speech at 10 p.m, much earlier than expected, and 'from first to last everything he said and did was in keeping — odd, eccentric, riskful, dangerous, desperate... [it was] the speech of wild genius.' There is indeed a suggestion that he had taken some dutch courage before he spoke, and he seems to have reverted to the slashing style of the days of his attacks on Peel — 'trampling, crushing, destroying all before him.' The House filled quickly as word got round of what was happening; there was much 'roaring and laughing' at Disraeli's retaliation against his numerous critics and people lost sight for a moment of the fact that this was unbecoming behaviour from the leader of the House of Commons. 'The House was lost in the wit, in the fun, in the savage, vindictive power of the orator.' However, when Disraeli sat down at around 1 a.m, the debate, instead of being concluded, was continued by Gladstone, who was resolved to make a reply. According to Whitty, Gladstone's face was 'full of fire, vigour and pluck', and he 'terrified people into silence':

> It was the dignified lofty rebuke from an honest, gifted nature of the impudent (there is no other word) outrage of Disraeli; and, as if by magic, that intense scorn which his voice and eye, rather than his language conveyed, altered the whole tone of the House, brought down a ringing, enduring cheer, and — changed the fate of the day.

Gladstone had crushed the Budget, and he had also urged the House, as a matter of self-respect, to rid itself of a government of tricksters. 'So much for character *with* genius, against genius only', was Whitty's verdict — admittedly a biased one — on this dramatic confrontation between political giants.[26]

As a result of the fall of the Conservatives, Lord Aberdeen, a Peelite, was invited to form a coalition government consisting of Liberals (including Russell and Palmerston), Gladstone and other Peelites, and a radical, Sir William Molesworth. This was obviously a great setback for those who had hoped that the Conservative party of Sir Robert Peel might be reconstructed. Derby was in no doubt that the Peelites' decision to join with the Liberals was 'mainly to be attributed to the jealousy & hatred (the word is not too strong) felt by the Peelite party in the House of Commons towards Disraeli.'[27] The clash between Disraeli and Gladstone over the Budget had served to widen the rift between Conservatives and Peelites, and it was now extremely doubtful whether it could ever be closed. Ironically, however, the consequent weakness of the Conservatives only made Disraeli's presence more indispensable to them, and it might almost have seemed as if Conservative failure was a precondition for his survival as the party's leader.

Opposition, 1853–8

It is certainly true that Disraeli was only tolerated by the Conservatives in the House of Commons because he was clearly subordinate to Derby, the acknowledged overall party 'chief'. Derby's patrician presence was reassuring to the country gentlemen on the backbenches, making it easier for them to accept the unavoidable necessity of Disraeli's leadership in the absence of any viable alternative candidate. Derby and Disraeli managed to work together for twenty years until Derby's retirement in 1868, but they were never very close personally (for instance, Derby would not condescend to visit Disraeli at Hughenden), and this serves to emphasise the extent to which theirs was a political relationship based on mutual dependence.[28] The period between the demise of Derby's first ministry and the formation of his second, in February 1858, was to see the greatest strains in the relationship between the two leaders, arising from their conflicting ideas about the appropriate strategy for an opposition party.[29]

Even in the early months of 1853, when the Aberdeen coalition was only barely established in office, there were abundant signs of Disraeli's resolve to bring the government down as quickly as possible. These sometimes took the form of direct attacks on Ministers, as in the case of his speech on foreign policy at the opening of the parliamentary session.[30] But Disraeli was also on the look-out for opportunities to prise apart the constituent elements of the coalition, in the hope that he could thus bring about a realignment of parliamentary forces. The most promising line of inquiry, in this respect, lay with the 'Whigs', that cadre of aristocratic Liberal administrators, among whom there was a good deal of dissatisfaction with the sacrifices of office required of them in order to facilitate the coalition with the Peelites. Disraeli speculated on the possibility that disgruntled Whigs excluded from the new government, like Sir George Grey and Lord Seymour, might be persuaded to coalesce with the Conservatives. A further point to be considered was that many Whigs, both in and out of the government, were known to be unhappy about Lord John Russell's plan for a new parliamentary reform bill, and it seemed to be on the cards that this issue might well wreck the Aberdeen coalition.[31] Indeed, at the end of 1853 Lord Palmerston temporarily resigned from the government over his opposition to Russell's scheme, and Derby's son, Lord Stanley, found Disraeli to be 'full of confidence & exultation, speculating on the juncture of Palmerston and the old Whigs generally with us, and on our having in consequence a numerical majority in the House.'[32] Palmerston's resignation was withdrawn at this point, but Disraeli's excitement with the political prospects was renewed when Russell introduced his Reform Bill in February 1854.

Disraeli was in private communication with a number of Whigs who disliked reform, and he still believed that the Conservatives could catch Palmerston too, as he explained to Stanley:

> Palmerston once gained, he felt sure of the rest: as to the lead, he was willing to give it up, P. being an old man, not capable of sustained exertion: the real power would always remain with himself, Disraeli. He exulted in the notion of revenge on Gladstone and the Peelites, who would be driven to Manchester, and must act under Bright.[33]

'Manchester' was a reference to the group of Radicals, including Richard Cobden and John Bright, who had successfully campaigned for Free Trade during the 1840s, through the vehicle of the Anti-Corn Law League (it was Disraeli who coined the phrase 'Manchester School' to describe them), and who therefore had some affinity with the Peelites.

Paradoxically, there were other occasions when Disraeli seemed interested in collaborating with those very same Radicals, who were not strongly committed to the support of Aberdeen's government and often took an independent line. Disraeli kept up a secret line of communication with the Radicals, and he was quite prepared to join with them suddenly in 'snap' divisions, sometimes succeeding in embarrassing the government as a result.[34] However, such behaviour horrified many Conservatives, who refused to vote with Disraeli, and he succeeded merely in reaffirming his reputation as an unscrupulous and unprincipled adventurer. Conservative distrust of Disraeli's unorthodox methods was also magnified by the appearance in May 1853 of a new weekly newspaper, *The Press*, with which Disraeli was known to be closely involved and which adopted a noticeably more 'liberal' tone than that of other Conservative papers. Dissatisfaction with Disraeli's opportunist political tactics, combined with the suspicions aroused by *The Press*, manifested themselves in the dismal Conservative showing on the government's India Bill in June 1853, when only 140 MPs (barely half of the party's parliamentary strength) bothered to support Disraeli's hostile amendment.[35]

The simple fact is that Disraeli was unpopular with many in his own party, who did not trust him. This was a cause of considerable concern to Derby, who felt that Disraeli needed to try harder to win his backbenchers' confidence by consulting them more.[36] Derby's own view was that it was better for the Opposition to adopt a more passive approach, avoiding gratuitous attacks on the government (which only served to drive ministers and their supporters closer together) and waiting for the undoubted internal fissures to work their way to the surface and bring about a spontaneous collapse. If the Aberdeen coalition could be seen to have failed through its own weaknesses, Derby believed the chances of an alternative parliamentary alignment, creating a working majority for a Derby administration, would be much more favourable. Derby's constant fear, however, was that his lieutenant in the House of Commons was much too restless to acquiesce in such a long-term strategy for obtaining power.[37]

When the Crimean War broke out in March 1854, it initially appeared that the Opposition was faced with a further period of political frustration. The immediate casualty of the war was Russell's Reform Bill, the abandonment of which put paid to Conservative hopes of a Whig secession from the Ministerial ranks. Furthermore, the Opposition risked being condemned as 'unpatriotic' if it tried to attack the government on any other issue: Disraeli, as one leading Conservative noted, was therefore 'furious with the war, which he thinks keeps Government in.'[38] But the war was soon to have a very different effect, as revelations were made about the incompetent management of the British expeditionary force, which left the troops to endure a winter in the Crimea without basic supplies. The Aberdeen coalition was discredited, and in January 1855 it suffered a humiliating defeat in the House of Commons, when a radical motion for a committee of inquiry into the conduct of the war was carried by the extraordinary margin of 305 votes to 148.

Derby was presented with what was ostensibly a marvellous opportunity to break the recent Liberal domination of government and establish a durable Conservative ministry. The reasons for his failure to do so are still a matter for dispute.[39] Following Aberdeen's resignation, Derby was invited to form a government; he proceeded (with Disraeli's consent) to offer the leadership of the Commons to Palmerston, on condition that two of the Peelites, Gladstone and Herbert, also agreed to join. Gladstone, however, who had been Chancellor of the Exchequer under Aberdeen, insisted on retaining this office, a demand which Disraeli considered unacceptable since it required him to efface himself twice over, which he was not prepared to do. The proposed ministerial arrangement therefore fell through, and Derby informed the Queen that he was unable to fulfil her commission. In a sense, it would be true to say that Disraeli was yet again the personal obstacle to the formation of a broadly-based Conservative government, but it is probable that Palmerston and Gladstone had pursued a course designed to ensure that Derby could not succeed. Palmerston realised that he had the game in his hands, and, benefiting as he did from the popular perception (fostered by much of the press) that he was the only man with the qualities to run the war properly, he was able to construct a government using most of the ingredients from the Aberdeen coalition.

There is a suspicion that Derby himself had not expected to be able to form a government immediately and that he was calculating on an early collapse of Palmerston's Ministry, either from the infirmity of the Premier (who was 70 years old) or through the proof, surely soon to be discovered by the public, that the new regime was as inefficient as its predecessor. Once Palmerston's incapacity for war leadership had been demonstrated, Derby anticipated that he would be in a position to form a strong government.[40] Derby's crime, in other words, was not that he was indifferent to office and gave up too easily, but that he miscalculated the likely achievements of a Palmerston ministry. With the benefit of hindsight, perhaps he should have followed Disraeli's advice and pressed on with a purely Conservative government after Palmerston and the Peelites declined to join him, but a minority government trying to conduct a war would have been in an extremely vulnerable position, unless military success had been quickly forthcoming. It is important to emphasise the genuine anger which Disraeli felt at what he regarded as Derby's admission of the Conservatives' incompetence to govern in a time of crisis, and for some time thereafter he was gloomy about the party's chances of political recovery. As he complained to Lord Malmesbury, in November 1855:

> We are off the rail of politics, and must continue so as long as the war lasts; and the only thing that can ever give us a chance is that the war should finish... Then we shall, at least, revert to the position we occupied before the fatal refusal to take the reins last February, which lost us the heart and respect of all Classes.[41]

In the years 1855–6 the fortunes of the Conservative party reached what was, even by its own mid-Victorian standards, surely the nadir. Palmerston's ministry proved to be far more resilient than anyone could have anticipated, even surviving the resignation of Gladstone and other leading Peelites, and by April 1856 it was able to end the war with Russia, convincing the British public that they had been victorious. The general Conservative distrust of Disraeli, meanwhile, was undiminished, especially after a misguided attempt late in 1855 to evolve a peace policy in conjunction with the Manchester Radicals. This episode naturally raised fresh doubts about Disraeli's political judgement, and he was firmly rebuked by Derby.[42] In fairness to Disraeli, the fact that he was a convenient hate-figure for many Conservative MPs may actually have served to deflect criticism away from Derby's undoubted shortcomings as a leader[43] — for the latter was often remote and inactive (partly the result of the painful attacks of gout to which he was prone). Whatever the case, a serious situation was allowed to develop during 1856 in which communications between the Conservative leaders in the Lords and the Commons virtually broke down. Derby even seems to have harboured suspicions that Disraeli was angling to have him deposed as the overall leader.[44] So worrying did matters become that the party whips felt obliged to take the initiative in demanding that some consultation between the leaders should take place before the start of the 1857 session in order to halt the spreading demoralisation within the Conservative ranks.[45] True, the session of 1857 opened more promisingly, and an opportunity arose for the Conservatives to align with dissident Liberals, Radicals and Peelites, in support of a motion censuring the government over the outbreak of the China war. But Palmerston responded to this censure by requesting a dissolution of parliament, so that he could appeal directly to the electorate. The outcome was that he gained a triumphant majority of 90 seats, while the Conservatives were reduced to a total of about 260, a net loss of twenty. Disraeli was forced to admit that, although the Conservatives had weathered the electoral storm reasonably well, it was clear that 'the hearts & humors of the very people, who supported us in the Country, are not very sunny towards us at this moment', and he concluded that any early confrontation with Palmerston's government was best avoided. Significantly, he was still disposed to blame Derby for the party's plight: 'It is useless to conceal it from ourselves, that the people of England have not forgiven, & probably never will forgive, the shrinking from responsibility in…1855…This is the root of all evil, & it is a very deep one.'[46]

Many Conservatives were perhaps more disposed to think of Disraeli as 'the root of all evil', and his continuing difficulties in trying to lead the party are well illustrated by the events of December 1857, when an emergency session of Parliament was summoned to discuss the banking crisis which threatened the stability of the financial markets. It was proposed by the Chancellor of the Exchequer, Cornewall Lewis, that a committee of inquiry should be set up, but Disraeli sought to exploit the crisis for partisan advantage by condemning the government for failing to make clear immediately what its policy was. In the division lobby, however, Disraeli was beaten by the embarrassing margin of 295 votes to 117. Colonel

Taylor, a junior whip, sounded out Conservative MPs afterwards and reported to the chief whip, Sir William Jolliffe, that 'all with whom I have spoken, without an exception, are angry, sulky, or otherwise dissatisfied with our division.' A large number of members had declined to attend for the vote, and Taylor felt that such evidence of the Opposition's disunion merely served to strengthen the government's position. He therefore urged Jolliffe to warn Disraeli of the damaging effects of his opportunistic approach to leadership, and concluded: '... however it may be adverse to his own inclinations to sit inactive on the front opposition bench, he has really not any choice left, but must if he cares for his own authority, and our continued existence, *bide his time.*'[47]

Palmerston's downfall, when it came in February 1858, was both sudden and bizarre, and in fact a triumph for the 'Disraelian' style of opportunist attack. The government had introduced a Conspiracy to Murder Bill, increasing the penalty for this offence, after it emerged that an assassination attempt on the Emperor of France had been planned by a group of Italian nationalists based in England. This measure was criticised as a craven response to threats from the French authorities — for once, ironically, Palmerston was accused of not being belligerent enough — and all the Premier's political enemies seized the tactical opportunity afforded by a cleverly-worded motion from the Radical, Milner Gibson, in order to inflict defeat on the government. Evidently, the decision by the Conservative leaders to support Milner Gibson was taken at the last minute.[48] To many observers of the political scene, Palmerston's consequent resignation seemed certain to mark the end of his long career, and, with Derby agreeing to form his second administration, the stage was set for an interesting experiment in Conservative government.

In search of 'Conservative Progress'

The similarities in the situation between Derby's ministry of 1858 and that of 1852 were so great as to suggest that its chances of long-term survival were poor. On both occasions, the Conservatives had found themselves in office as a result of the quarrels among their opponents, and they did not possess an overall majority in the House of Commons. In February 1858, as in February 1852, Derby was unable to attract support from beyond the Conservative ranks: Earl Grey, a semi-detached Whig, and the Peelites, Gladstone, Herbert and the Duke of Newcastle, all declined the invitations made to them (Gladstone also refused a further offer made in May). Derby's son, Lord Stanley, when listing his reasons for thinking the new government could not last for more than one parliamentary session, touched upon a major source of weakness: 'the character of Disraeli, who must lead the Commons, does not command general confidence, either in Parliament or among the public. If in difficulty, he would probably resort to desperate expedients...whence might arise differences between him and the Premier.'[49] Such was the verdict of Disraeli's closest colleague in the Commons.

If the government was intrinsically weak, there was also the problem of finding a suitable course of policy for it to pursue. What had emerged from the politics of the past dozen years was the impossibility of the Conservatives trying to operate on purely traditional 'Tory' lines. Protectionism, of course, had long since been abandoned, and little was heard by 1858 of the 'paternalistic' social concerns which Disraeli and others had articulated in the 1840s. There was little alternative, apparently, but for the Conservatives to use their spell in office (which was likely to be brief) to begin to build a reputation for moderate government and administrative efficiency along essentially Liberal-Peelite lines. For a time, the idea of 'Conservative Progress', enunciated in a speech by Derby, became the key political slogan for the party.

In fact, the legislative performance of Derby's second ministry was far from negligible. The most important measure to be carried in 1858 was the Government of India Act, transferring power from the East India Company to the Crown, a step rendered necessary by the mutiny in India the previous year. It did not matter that the Act, in the form in which it was eventually passed, was more or less identical to the one proposed by Palmerston's government before its resignation: the Conservatives could still justifiably claim the credit for having settled the issue. Other useful reforms dealt with by the government related to public health and to the Scottish universities. At the same time, the Conservatives allowed to pass into law the Bill introduced by a radical, Peter Locke King, to abolish the property qualifications for MPs. Perhaps the most instructive episode of all, during the 1858 session, concerned the Oaths Bill, designed to allow Jews to sit in parliament. The government blocked Lord John Russell's Bill, as it obviously did not want to see an opponent gain the plaudits for legislating on the subject, but it then acquiesced in an alternative Bill brought forward by a Conservative peer, Lord Lucan. With a modest record of legislative achievement behind them, all the signs were that the Conservatives had more good work in preparation for the 1859 session. As a radical MP, Sir John Trelawny, realised, 'The game of the Derby Cabinet is to present themselves in the guise of Administrative Reformers — with their budget of measures ready for use', and when Bills to deal with bankruptcy and highways were introduced Trelawny jokingly remarked that 'The Whig hacks must be frantic. Why, good god! the country may learn, if this goes on, to forget the value of Whig government.'[50] In the event, however, a dissolution of parliament was to intervene before these plans could be implemented.

Disraeli's contribution to 'Conservative Progress' appears to be comparatively slight, but it is possible that if the government had survived longer his projected budget for 1859 might well have earned him considerable credit. The striking thing about Disraeli's attitude to financial policy, by the late 1850s, is the extent to which he had absorbed 'Peelite' orthodoxies. In his stopgap Budget for 1858, introduced not long after the Conservatives had entered office, he took advantage of a healthy surplus by reducing the rate of income tax from 7d. to 5d. (there was no talk now of differentiation), with a view to its complete abolition in 1860 — precisely the objective laid down in Gladstone's first Budget of 1853. If Disraeli had been able to present his 1859 Budget it would have been an ambitious scheme, intended to propel the government forward, containing two impeccably orthodox Free Trade provisions: the reduction of the duty on tea and the abolition of the duty on paper.[51] (The latter measure was to bring Gladstone much political prestige when he enacted it in 1861.) Convinced of the political virtues of low taxation, Disraeli had fought an almost 'Gladstonian' battle within the Cabinet to resist demands for increased expenditure on the navy.

The final monument to 'Conservative Progress' was the government's Parliamentary Reform Bill, introduced by Disraeli in February 1859. Contrary to appearance, he had had grave doubts about the wisdom of this measure, and it was Derby who provided the necessary impetus to bring the Bill forward. At first sight, an attempt by the Conservatives to settle an issue which had been prominent for over a decade, since the collapse of the last Chartist demonstration, might have seemed a bold initiative with the potential to greatly enhance the party's reputation. In reality, though, the Reform Bill merely demonstrated the limitations of the Conservatives as a serious party of 'liberal' government. The Bill went too far for two Cabinet Ministers, J. W. Henley and Spencer Walpole, who resigned in protest. And yet the government's opponents quickly perceived that the measure was essentially an exercise in electoral gerrymandering: a £10 household franchise was proposed for the counties, to bring them into line with the boroughs (the sticking point for Henley and Walpole), but this was unlikely to cause much disturbance in constituencies that were already Conservative strongholds. The borough franchise was not to be lowered, as many Liberals wanted, but a number of so-called 'fancy franchises' were to be added, conferring votes on certain professional groups, as well as on those with £60 in the savings bank, those with an income of £10 or more from the Funds, and so on. It was estimated that the total borough electorate would thus have been increased by a modest 200,000, and the aim was evidently to confine the additional borough voters to social groups who might be better disposed towards the Conservative party, thereby creating an opportunity for some inroads to be made into traditional Liberal territory. Finally, a redistribution of seats from small to large boroughs was proposed, but on an extremely limited scale, affecting a mere fifteen small boroughs.[52]

Predictably enough, the Conservatives' Reform Bill was so modest in its scope, and so obviously designed to extract what little extra electoral advantage was available to the party within the existing structure, that its effect was to unite the Liberals, Radicals and Peelites in common opposition. Even Palmerston, a lukewarm reformer, had no difficulty in joining in the attack. When the Bill was defeated in April Derby obtained a dissolution of Parliament, and at the ensuing general election the Conservatives succeeded in recovering the losses of 1857, emerging roughly 300 strong. This was not a bad result, but common antipathy to a Conservative government meant that their opponents were able to coalesce (at the famous Willis's Rooms meeting of 6 June 1859) and subsequently carry a vote of no confidence in the Ministry. The long period of political confusion initiated by the Corn Law crisis of 1846 was brought to an end at last, with Palmerston forming a comprehensive Liberal ministry including Russell, Gladstone and other Peelites, and some radical representatives, which survived until the Premier's death in October 1865. All of Derby's efforts to piece together a Conservative majority by drawing on the floating body of 'moderate' opinion had come to nothing, a fact that was at least partly explicable in terms of the 'repellent' effect of his House of Commons lieutenant, which he had recognised ten years earlier.

Opposition, 1859–65

In a private letter written in December 1856, Derby had provided an acute analysis of the dilemmas facing the Conservative Party while in opposition to a Palmerston ministry. Palmerston was, Derby knew, at heart a 'Conservative Minister...working with Radical tools', a feat he achieved through a display of patriotism in his foreign policy. By acting in such a distinctive way, Palmerston was able to avoid 'making any attacks upon our institutions', and this left the Conservatives with little ground for opposing him: it was hardly possible to convince the public that the Monarchy, the Church or the House of Lords was under threat from a Palmerston regime.[53] After June 1859 Derby and Disraeli were to be confronted with similar tactical problems, and they enjoyed no greater success in devising an effective counter to Palmerston's style of leadership.

It there was a difference in the Conservatives' approach to Opposition after 1859, it lay in a greater readiness on Disraeli's part to accept the validity of Derby's strategy of refraining from unnecessary attacks on the government. Of course, this did not mean that the Opposition never challenged Palmerston: the most notable exception came in July 1864, when Disraeli's motion censuring the government's inept diplomacy in the Schleswig-Holstein crisis was defeated by only 313 votes to 295 in a virtually straight-party fight. It was much more often the case, though, that even when the Conservatives were critical of the government they were wary of becoming involved in tests of party strength in the division lobbies. For a brief period, in the sessions of 1860 and 1861, there was actually a secret understanding between Derby and Palmerston whereby Derby promised not to oppose the government if it was endangered by pressure from the Radicals on issues like parliamentary reform. The offer also applied in the event of the Chancellor of the Exchequer, Gladstone, who was in conflict with the Premier over financial policy, deciding to resign and join with the Radicals. Interestingly, Disraeli was prepared to accede to this arrangement.[54] Derby's motive for offering a temporary truce in party warfare was not that he had given up hope of regaining power for himself, but that he believed the best way of undermining Palmerston was by encouraging him to stick to moderate policies, as this was bound to increase the frustration of his more radical colleagues and backbenchers, and must eventually provoke an internal Liberal collapse. By supporting Palmerston, in other words, Derby was trying to destroy him: as in the 1850s, he perceived that the worst mistake the Opposition could make would be to indulge in factious attacks on Ministers, as these had the inevitable psychological effect of drawing the Liberals closer together.[55] We therefore find Disraeli, prior to the 1861 session, anticipating a quiet time, but also predicting the future disruption of the Liberal Party and a possible fusion between the Conservatives and 'Whigs' like Sir George Grey, Sir George Cornewall Lewis, and Lord Clarendon. He was confident that 'the quarrel between Whigs and ultras [i.e. Radicals] is irreconcilable.'[56]

Unfortunately for Derby's and Disraeli's calculations, Palmerston was much too adroit to allow himself to fall into the trap set for him. He was certainly quite happy to make use of Conservative assistance when it suited him (for instance, to block inconvenient radical initiatives on Parliamentary Reform) but he was also careful to make enough concessions, notably to Gladstone over finance, to prevent any permanent rift from opening up. Indeed, Palmerston's room for manoeuvre was increased by the evident unwillingness of many Conservative country gentlemen to see his government disturbed, which meant that on the few occasions when Disraeli did seek a little political adventure he was unable to command the unanimous support of his own backbenchers. Thus, in May 1861 an opportunity arose for Disraeli to align with disgruntled Irish MPs in opposition to Gladstone's Bill to repeal the paper duties, but the attack failed because some twenty Conservatives deliberately absented themselves, not wishing to be associated with such an unprincipled alliance. Some idea of the Conservatives' discontent with their leader's conduct is conveyed by the diary of Thomas Sotheron-Estcourt (a Minister in the 1858–9 government), who recorded how, a few days after the division, 'Cayly, Holford, Mitford [all backbenchers] took me aside to talk about the schism in the party.' He found that 'Distrust of Disraeli. Fear of Change of Government', were the prevailing sentiments. Two days later

Sotheron-Estcourt noted that Sir John Pakington, a front bench Conservative, also 'confided to me his dissatisfaction with Disraeli.'[57] Similarly, in June 1862, a Disraelian-inspired attempt to attack the government for its excessive expenditure — an issue likely to attract support from the Radicals — collapsed when Palmerston made it clear that he regarded the vote as one of confidence. Afterwards, Sotheron-Estcourt found 'our people very sulky...Heathcote [a senior back-bencher] sat with me — very angry — says further action with Dizzy is impossible.' A week later Sotheron-Estcourt had a long interview with Disraeli, who 'gave me an elaborate statement of the difficulties of his position...Only two alternatives. Either confidence must be given or he retires.' Once more, Sotheron-Estcourt found himself required to play the part of peacemaker.[58]

The extraordinary fact is that, even after some fifteen years as Conservative leader in the House of Commons, it was still doubtful whether Disraeli would be acceptable to the party as its overall chief in the event of Derby's disappearance from the political scene.[59] Some of the 'High Tories', who detested Disraeli on social and personal as well as political grounds, were actively plotting to have him removed from his post in the autumn of 1863.[60] Early in the following year, Lord Stanley recorded that 'The party of malcontents on the Conservative side now numbers about twenty-five, and has the sympathies of many more.' The ringleader was G. W. P. Bentinck ('Big Ben'), and his associates included Lord Robert Cecil, the future Prime Minister (as Lord Salisbury). The two Cabinet Ministers who had resigned over the Reform Bill of 1859, Henley and Walpole, were apparently giving this group encouragement.[61] It was fortunate for Disraeli that there was no obvious candidate for his place, someone who might have been able to cultivate the support of these troublesome backbenchers.

There is a natural tendency for us to think of Disraeli at this stage in his career as still a relatively young man, but the reality was that he reached the age of sixty in December 1864. He had held high office on two occasions, but only very briefly, and it was far from certain that he would achieve much more, given the almost permanently entrenched position of the Conservatives as the party of Opposition. The likelihood of Disraeli reaching the highest office of all would have seemed remote. Unsurprisingly, perhaps, the man who is often credited with inventing the concept of opposition for opposition's sake was showing signs of losing his appetite for the political game. In February 1865, Lord Stanley observed that 'Disraeli's increasing apathy to public affairs is becoming a subject of general remark: I have myself noticed it for the last two or three years.' Disraeli's age and the unpromising political outlook were obvious explanations, but Stanley also thought there was the old problem of the 'occasional difficulty in acting with Ld D[erby] between whom and him there is no very cordial feeling'.[62] It is not often appreciated just how inactive Disraeli became, but a good indication is provided by his voting record in the House of Commons: of 188 divisions taking place during the 1863 session, Disraeli's name appears in only eight; in 1864 he voted in seventeen out of 156 divisions, and in 1865 just nine times out of a possible 104. Only with the death of Palmerston, in October 1865, would Disraeli display signs of renewed vigour.[63]

The state of political torpor characterising the final years of Palmerston's ascendancy may also help to account for an intriguing aspect of Disraeli's personal life which has only recently come to light. Evidence has emerged to suggest that in the mid-1860s he fathered two illegitimate children: Ralph Nevill (born March 1865), whose mother was Lady Dorothy Nevill, a close friend and neighbour of the Disraelis, and Kate Donovan (born March 1866), whose mother's identity is unknown. Kate could well have been the mysterious 'infant beneficiary' referred to some years later by Disraeli's executors as having been discreetly omitted from his will.[64] If Disraeli was indeed the father of these children (and we cannot be absolutely sure about this), their conception would certainly have coincided with a low point in his life: Mary Anne, his wife, was ageing and often in poor health but, above all, politics was not providing him with an adequate distraction from other matters.

Disraeli and the House of Commons

We have seen how precarious Disraeli's position in the House of Commons continued to be, even as late as 1865, and it has been emphasised that he owed his survival as leader to his skill in debate. The mid-Victorian Conservative party was confronted by a formidable debating force on the opposing side, which included Palmerston and Russell together with Peelites such as Gladstone, Herbert and Sir James Graham, as well as Radicals like Roebuck, Cobden and Bright. Disraeli was really the only Conservative in the lower House capable of competing with speakers of this calibre, and, for all the carping that went on in the benches behind him, it could hardly be denied that he was an invaluable asset to his party. It therefore seems appropriate to conclude this chapter with a brief discussion of how Disraeli appeared to contemporary observers when he was in his natural political habitat, the House of Commons.

By far the best account of Disraeli's parliamentary manner is provided by William White, the doorkeeper of the House of Commons, who contributed a weekly column to the *Illustrated Times*. Describing the scene as it might have been in the lobby, at 4 or 5 p.m. on the day of a major debate, White wrote that Disraeli 'comes up the members' private staircase, marches across the lobby, solemnly and slowly, generally alone, and speaking to no one as he passes.' On entering the chamber, he 'sits down, folds his arms across his breast, and keeps immovably in this position, with his eyes fixed upon the ground, until he rises to speak.' Disraeli was unusual in that he never wore his hat while in the chamber, whereas most Members found that item rather useful for concealing their emotions from their fellows:

> But Disraeli needs no hat, for he neither winces nor laughs and seldom cheers; in fact, he sits like an imperturbable statue. His place is between Napier and Walpole or Whiteside, but he seldom speaks to his neighbours. Though in the midst of his party, he appears not to be of them, but is as separate and distinct as his race is from all the world.

If possible, Disraeli liked to make the closing speech of the debate, and he therefore often did not commence until after midnight. White thought that visitors who had come specially to hear Disraeli speak were often disappointed, or at least surprised, to find that he was not a magnificent orator (in White's view, no one in the House of Commons in 1856 merited that description):

> When he rises he generally starts bolt upright, then leans his hands upon the table, and casts his eyes downwards. At first he not infrequently hesitates and stammers a good deal, shambling like an old mail-coach horse who has got stiff by standing in the stall, but, like the said coach-horse, he soon warms up to his work. He then takes his hands off the table, thrusts them it may be into his waistcoat-pocket, and turns his face towards the House; or else, if he feels well up, he folds his arms across his breast. Then he hesitates no more, but his sentences come out in stately flow. Disraeli's sentences are specially remarkable for their excellent English, and for the peculiar appropriateness of his words, especially of his adjectives. If there is an adjective in the language especially suitable to express his meaning, that he will be sure to use. But still he generally disappoints, for the first three-quarters of an hour, strangers who hear him for the first time. There is nothing witty, nothing specially brilliant, for it is his peculiarity that he reserves all his wit and brilliancy until he is about to finish; and those who are used to him well know when it is coming. He shifts his position, turning with his face towards the Treasury Bench, and heralds the coming witticism by a slight curl of the mouth and twinkle of the eyes. And then for about a quarter of an hour, if he be quite himself and the occasion is favourable, it is seen that he still possesses that power of sarcasm and wit which so galled Sir Robert Peel in the Corn Law struggle.[65]

The Radical MP Sir John Trelawny recorded in his diary how Disraeli's countenance, on sitting down after one of his more triumphant attacks on Palmerston's second Ministry, reminded him of a 'vivacious viper'.[66]

Since joining the Conservative frontbench in 1846 Disraeli had presented a more sober image to his audience, no longer indulging in dandified forms of dress and usually being clothed instead all in black. Yet there remained about him an aura of mystery, a sense of his differentness from his Conservative colleagues, which is confirmed by the journalist E. M. Whitty, writing in 1853. Whitty described Disraeli as 'the least English-looking man I ever saw' (he was contrasting him with the Radical, John Bright), and suggested that whereas Bright was a successful debater because he was 'so intensely English, earnest, and natural', Disraeli was 'a House of Commons hero, because he is so magnificent an actor, so superbly historical and impartial, and so elegantly artificial.' Likening Disraeli to his own fictional creation, Sidonia, in the Young England trilogy, who maintained that a Jewish gentleman had the great advantage of being a gentleman without a country, Whitty felt that it was the impression of emotional detachment which gave 'a strange power to Mr Disraeli as a speaker in the House of Commons.'[67]

As a parliamentary tactician, Disraeli possessed a well-earned reputation for deviousness. Trelawny recorded that one of Disraeli's favourite devices was 'flying kites', namely the trick of 'putting members up to take the chance of making a successful attack on Ministers & then not sharing the responsibility to the length of recommending them to go to a division.'[68] On one occasion, when the rising young Conservative MP Sir Stafford Northcote launched an offensive against Gladstone's financial policy, Trelawny noted how Disraeli contrived to speak last, by temporarily leaving the chamber, so that Gladstone was obliged to rise before the Speaker closed the debate by putting the question. Shortly after Gladstone had commenced, Disraeli 'glided in, like a snake', later apologising for his accidental absence. Trelawny's verdict was blunt: 'Rogue, this was regularly preconcerted, no doubt. Northcote drew the badger, & then his leader assailed it when at a disadvantage. Tricky business this — & wrong if only because transparent!'[69]

These comments by observers who had seen Disraeli at first hand reveal much about the general opinion of the man. In particular, his foreignness (and more specifically his Jewishness) are frequently emphasised: this was a source of political strength in some respects, but at the same time a reminder that he was still regarded as a social intruder in an assembly of gentlemen. And it is noteworthy that on two separate occasions Trelawny used the image of the serpent when describing Disraeli. It seems that he managed both to intrigue his contemporaries and to fill them with a sense of moral danger.

3

CONSTRUCTING THE 'TORY DEMOCRACY'

Introduction

The task of political reconstruction facing Disraeli and the mid-Victorian Conservative party is brought out very clearly in the following table, which lists the General Election returns for 1859. This represented the best Conservative performance at the polls in the period between the Corn Law crisis of 1846 and the triumph of 1874.[1]

The General Election of 1859

		Conservatives	Others
English	Counties	99	45
	Boroughs	117	203
	Universities	4	0
Welsh	Counties	10	5
	Boroughs	6	8
Scottish	Counties	15	15
	Burghs	0	23
Irish	Counties	34	30
	Boroughs	19	20
	University	2	0
UK Total		306	348

With slightly more than one-half of all Conservative seats being held in county constituencies, the party's continued identification with the landed interest was obvious. In fact, that association was much more powerful than the county figures alone suggest, because most of the borough seats won by Conservative candidates had small electorates and were substantially rural in their social character. Of the 117 Conservative borough seats in England, 86 (out of a possible 198) were in constituencies with less than 1,000 voters, 23 (of a possible 63) were in middling-size constituencies of 1–2,000, voters, while a mere eight (of a possible 59) were in large constituencies with over 2,000 voters.[2] There could never be any question, given this distribution of Conservative electoral strength, of the party leaders deliberately abandoning or diluting their commitment to the defence of landed society, and they would have had no wish to do so in any case, but it was also apparent that if the Conservatives were ever to cease to be the 'natural' party of opposition, as they had been since 1846, they needed to supplement their traditional sources of support.

For many years Derby and Disraeli had sought to encourage some of the more moderate Liberals to desert their party and join the Conservatives. Such a realignment of parliamentary forces would have given the Conservatives an even greater concentration of power in their natural strongholds, the counties and rural boroughs, but this desirable outcome was never to be achieved either in Derby's or Disraeli's lifetime. An alternative approach, not incompatible with the luring of moderate Liberals, was to emphasise the responsible, reformist credentials of the Conservative party in the hope of gaining some additional support in the middling and larger boroughs. However, on the crucial political battleground of finance, it was Gladstone rather than Disraeli who emerged triumphant after 1859. As Chancellor of the Exchequer in Palmerston's ministry, Gladstone embarked upon a further extension of the principles of Free Trade, and within a few years the economy had grown so rapidly, and the government's revenue from the few remaining tariffs was so buoyant, that it became permissible for him to reduce the burden of income tax. By 1865 he had managed to lower the rate to just 4d. (less than 2p) in the pound. It may have been true, as we saw in the last chapter, that Disraeli's thinking on financial policy had developed along remarkably similar lines during the 1850s, but the fact remains that it was Gladstone who implemented the policies and he and the Liberal party who gained the political credit for them. In these circumstances, the Liberals' customary domination of the urban constituencies appeared to be virtually unchallengeable.

Not until 1874 would the Conservatives succeed in breaking out of their electoral straitjacket, making significant gains in the urban centres and achieving an overall majority in the House of Commons. Before then, Derby was to experience for the third time the dubious pleasures of conducting a minority administration, which lasted from June 1866 until his retirement in February 1868. Disraeli succeeded him as Prime Minister, but his tenure of the highest office lasted only ten months. The Conservative breakthrough of 1874, which finally placed Disraeli in a position of real power, is traditionally associated with his adumbration of the principles of what later became known as 'Tory Democracy', most famously in his public speeches at Manchester and the Crystal Palace, in April and June of 1872. Here, it seems, Disraeli was successfully evolving a version of his Young England ideas of the 1840s, modified to suit the requirements of an increasingly prosperous, urbanised and industrialised society that was wedded to certain basic Liberal values.

It is important to emphasise the point that there was very little new in Disraeli's speeches of 1872. Rather, the process of repackaging his political ideas had been going on since the beginning of the 1860s, but it took some years, and a change in circumstances, before he caught the electorate's eye and convinced them that what he had to offer was a relevant response to the perceived problems of the time. As early as August 1862 a Radical MP noted how, during a House of Commons debate, Disraeli 'boldly adopted the name of

"Tory"': in fact, he had declared that 'Tory' principles were 'to uphold the institutions of the Country', an almost identical form of words to those used in his public speeches a decade later.[3] In an address to a Conservative Party dinner in June 1863, Disraeli again foreshadowed his Manchester and Crystal Palace speeches by denouncing the sinister aims of the Liberal Party, which, he alleged, included the introduction of a democratic franchise, an attack on property rights, Church disestablishment, and the severing of the links between Britain and her colonies. For his own party, Disraeli characteristically asserted its claims to be the true 'national' party:

> The Tory party is only in its proper position when it represents popular principles. Then it is truly irresistible. Then it can uphold the throne and the altar, the majesty of the empire, the liberty of the nation, and the rights of the multitude. There is nothing mean, petty or exclusive about the real character of Toryism. It necessarily depends upon enlarged sympathies and noble aspirations, because it is essentially national.[4]

Unsurprisingly, Disraeli's indictment of Liberalism was to prove far more effective when levelled against the party of Gladstone than it was against the party of Palmerston (who remained Prime Minister until his death in October 1865). Nevertheless, it is worth examining in turn the various elements in Disraeli's updated 'Toryism' — the Church, the Crown, the empire, and the question of parliamentary reform — which eventually merged into a formidable critique of the Gladstonian Liberal party of the early 1870s.

Church and Queen

One aspect of Disraeli's political career in the 1860s which has attracted surprisingly little attention from his modern biographers is his attempt to pose as the champion of the established Anglican Church.[5] In a letter to a colleague written in February 1861, Disraeli went so far as to assert that 'in internal politics, there is only one question now, the maintenance of the Church. There can be no refraining or false Liberalism on such a subject.'[6] The main threat to the Church of England at this time came from the activities of a nonconformist pressure group, the Liberation Society, whose ultimate objective was disestablishment — to place the Anglicans on an equal footing with the other religious denominations. As an interim measure, however, the Liberation Society focused much of its campaigning energy on securing the abolition of Church Rates — a long-standing grievance in parishes where nonconformist householders were in a minority, as they could be legally compelled to pay a rate levied by the local vestry for the purpose of maintaining the fabric of the parish church. Ominously for the Church of England, a bill for the simple abolition of Church Rates, introduced by a Radical MP on behalf of the Liberation Society, was passed by the House of Commons in 1858 and had to be killed off in the Lords. It therefore seemed essential in Disraeli's view that the friends of the Church should rally to its defence, and, when the Church Rates abolition bill came before the Commons in 1860, the strong line taken against it by Disraeli helped to secure a reduction in the second-reading majority (29, compared with 53 in 1858). Once again, however, the Conservatives had to rely on the upper House to block the measure.

At a diocesan meeting at Amersham in his Buckinghamshire constituency, in December 1860, Disraeli delivered a speech amounting to a Church defence manifesto. He argued against any compromise on the Church Rates issue, preferring to see the established Church stand up for its legal rights. The suggestion made by some moderate Conservatives that the matter should be resolved by allowing nonconformists to claim exemption from payment of the rate was rejected by Disraeli on the grounds that this would be a fatal admission that the Church was no longer the Church of the whole nation, and that this would serve to strengthen the Liberation Society in the pursuit of its real goal, disestablishment. Disraeli therefore urged his audience to sink their doctrinal differences and unite to form new Church defence organisations in order to counter the nonconformist agitation. With much greater exertion on the part of the Church's supporters, and with the consequent stiffening in the resolve of many MPs, it proved possible to swing the political balance against the Church Rates Abolition Bill, which was defeated in the House of Commons by increasing margins during the sessions of 1861–3.

Disraeli made several other appearances at Church gatherings in the early 1860s as he sought to exploit the full political potential from his apparently fertile new theme. Speaking at Aylesbury in November 1861, he offered a defence of the principle of Church establishment in language strongly reminiscent of his Young England days. The Church was 'a majestic corporation — wealthy, powerful, independent — with the sanctity of a long tradition', but happily it had been willing to defer to the civil power of the State, and thus the two had formed a formidable partnership, working for social order rather than entering into a destructive competition for supremacy. 'Broadly and deeply planted in the land, mixed up with all of the prime securities of our common liberties, the Church of England is part of our history, part of our life, part of England itself.' The following year, at Wycombe, Disraeli reiterated his belief in the value of Church establishment and called on the Anglicans to assert their nationality by working, through such means as improved provision for elementary education, in order to win the allegiance and shape the moral character of the millions of British citizens who — as the famous religious census of 1851 had shown — were indifferent to organised religion. Emphasising once again the integral part played by the Church of England in forming the national identity, Disraeli declared: 'Industry, Liberty, Religion — that *is* the history of England.'

In fact, Disraeli made the defence of the Church the first item in his general election address, issued in the summer of 1865. Unfortunately for him, the electorate did not seem to feel the same sense of urgency about religious questions. After all, the moderate Liberal regime of Palmerston was still in place, and in any case the nonconformist campaign against

Church Rates had lost much of its momentum.[7] The 1865 general election was probably the quietest of Victoria's reign, and the Conservatives lost ground slightly compared with their improved performance of 1859. While the 'Church in danger' cry proved ineffective on this occasion, Disraeli was to continue to utilise it at subsequent elections and eventually reaped some political reward for his efforts.

It may seem surprising that one can write of Disraeli and the Conservatives attaching themselves to the Crown during the course of the 1860s, since this would appear to be a natural and permanent relationship. Certainly we may recall that in his Young England trilogy of the 1840s Disraeli had advocated the restoration of the powers of the Crown. And yet, in the aftermath of the Corn Law crisis, those Conservatives who repudiated Peel's leadership became painfully aware that they had also forfeited the trust of their monarch. Queen Victoria, influenced by her consort, Prince Albert, was deeply attached to Peel for what she regarded as his disinterested statesmanship, and after his death in 1850 the royal couple were active in encouraging a coalition between the Peelites and the Liberals. True, Victoria and Albert were less than enthusiastic about the Liberal leaders, Russell and Palmerston, but it did not follow that Derby and Disraeli, the very men who had destroyed Peel's government, were considered to be desirable alternatives. Of course, there was never any question of the Conservatives adopting a hostile line against the Crown, but nor could they plausibly claim to be a party identified with it in any special way. In the early 1860s, however, the first signs began to appear of a relaxing in royal attitudes, particularly towards Disraeli, who still suffered from his reputation as an unscrupulous adventurer. Disraeli and his wife received their first invitation to stay at Windsor Castle, in January 1861, which was an important social breakthrough. More significantly, after the death of Albert in December 1861, Disraeli earned the Queen's gratitude for his generous public tribute to the high character of the Prince (sentiments that were probably quite genuine), and for his subsequent support for the Albert Memorial project. In March 1863 Disraeli and Mary Anne were favoured with an invitation to the wedding of the Prince of Wales and Princess Alexandra of Denmark, and in the following month he received a personal audience from the Queen, an honour normally reserved for government ministers.[8]

Consequently, by the time Disraeli became Prime Minister in 1868 he had already succeeded in cultivating a good relationship with the Queen, and this was quickly to become very cordial. Disraeli always preferred the company of women — throughout his career, most of his political confidants were female — and he knew instinctively how to establish a close personal rapport with his sovereign, breaking down the formal barriers of protocol. There can be no doubt that the chivalric tone in which he addressed the Queen, and the elaborate flattery he employed, were at least in part a deliberate strategy designed to win royal favour, but it must be remembered that the constitutional powers of the Crown were far from extinct and could not be disregarded by the Prime Minister, who naturally therefore wished to have the Queen as an ally. Moreover, Disraeli's sympathetic management of the Queen was astute in that, since the death of her husband, Victoria had often been difficult to deal with and sometimes almost hysterical. The advantages Disraeli gained from his skilful handling of the Queen become obvious when we consider the difficulties experienced by his great rival, Gladstone, whose stiff manner and lack of personal finesse soon alienated Victoria.[9] Interestingly, Disraeli expressed private concern that the Queen, by her almost total seclusion from public life since 1861, was throwing away her popularity, and diminishing the prestige of the monarchy.[10] Such fears eventually proved to be groundless, though, and the emotional bond between the Crown and the Conservative party was to become a tremendous political asset for Disraeli in the 1870s.

The Empire

Disraeli's attitude towards the British Empire has often been misunderstood. The prominence which he gave to this subject in his Crystal Palace speech of 1872 encouraged the later belief, particularly strong amongst writers hostile to Disraeli, that he was heralding a new era of aggressive imperialism which contrasted sharply with his earlier lack of interest in the colonies, proving once again that he was merely an opportunist. In support of this interpretation it was possible to point to a number of instances in the mid-Victorian era when Disraeli appeared to be expressing anti-imperial sentiments — most notoriously of all, his reference in 1852 to 'Those wretched colonies...[which] are a millstone round our necks.'[11] However, it is necessary to set such comments into their immediate context. It then becomes clear that Disraeli, as Chancellor of the Exchequer, was expressing momentary irritation at the financial burden imposed upon Britain by the cost of defending her colonies and at the complications in British foreign policy sometimes caused by her colonial commitments — specifically, in the case of his 1852 outburst, the way that relations with the USA were being strained because of a fisheries dispute between the USA and Canada. From a more general perspective, it can be argued that Disraeli actually displayed a consistent concern with the importance of maintaining the Empire, which he regarded as an essential pillar supporting Britain's status as a great power in the eyes of the world. This belief was made apparent as early as 1836, in his 'Runnymede' letters, published in *The Times* (see above, p. 14).[12]

Speaking in a House of Commons debate in July 1862, Disraeli launched an attack on Liberal colonial policy which was remarkably similar in content to his critique of Gladstonian policy at the Crystal Palace ten years later. On both occasions, when Disraeli referred to 'the colonies' he meant the countries populated by white settlers of British origin, namely Canada, Australia, New Zealand, and parts of Southern Africa. Disraeli condemned the Liberals in 1862 for having allowed hasty arrangements to be made for self-government in the white colonies without giving proper thought to such questions as their commercial relations with the mother country and their obligations for providing their own defence. In other words, Disraeli was expressing regret that an opportunity had been missed for binding Britain and her colonies closer together.[13] Nevertheless, he still hoped that by encouraging the colonies to accept responsibility for their defence, and thus removing a major British grievance, it might yet be possible for imperial ties to be strengthened. That this was desirable, from Britain's point of view, Disraeli had no doubt: 'I think a great empire, founded on sound principles of freedom and equality, is as conducive to the spirit and power of a community as commercial prosperity or military force.'[14]

It has been suggested by one historian that the Abyssinian war of 1867–8 marked the beginning of a new phase of British imperial expansion, and that it was this episode that convinced Disraeli of the rich political potential in such a policy.[15] The war was prompted by the bizarre behaviour of the mentally unstable Emperor Theodore of Abyssinia (now Ethiopia), who had seized a number of British officials and missionaries working in his country and imprisoned them in chains in his castle at Magdala. With British public opinion enraged by Theodore's conduct, Derby's Ministry was obliged to respond by ordering the despatch of a military force from India, which achieved a brilliant success in securing the release of the British prisoners without suffering a single fatality (Theodore committed suicide). Once the war was over, in June 1868, Disraeli, now the Prime Minister, was able to celebrate the exploits of an expedition that had 'elevated the military...character of England throughout the world.' It mattered little that the cost to the taxpayer amounted to £9 million, rather than the original estimate of £5 million. Significantly, however, Britain did not annex Abyssinia but simply installed a more friendly Emperor; and she subsequently showed no economic interest in the country, leaving the way open for the Italians to set up a trading company there. The Abyssinian war was hardly a manifestation of the 'new imperialism', therefore, but rather an assertion of British military strength — a triumphant defence of the nation's *prestige* in the eyes of the rest of the world — and this was the valuable political lesson that Disraeli learned from the affair.

Parliamentary reform

At the time the Conservative Ministers ordered the military expedition to Abyssinia they had almost completed the passage through Parliament of a remarkable measure of reform which confounded many of their Liberal opponents. The second Reform Act of 1867 would, in retrospect, play an important part in shaping the Conservative Party's sense of its own identity, confirming, as it appeared to do, the belief that the Conservatives were the 'national' party. Disraeli himself was to make a crucial contribution to the perpetuation of this Conservative myth about the events of 1867, as we shall see. But in reality the Reform Act was not the product of a preconceived plan on Disraeli's (or anyone else's) part, inspired by a belief in the conservatism of the masses; it can properly be understood only as an improvised measure, the details of which were largely dependent on the tactical situation facing Disraeli in the House of Commons.

Parliamentary Reform in 1867, after all, was implemented by a *minority* Conservative government, still headed at this stage by Derby, which had come into office in June 1866 as a result of the Liberal party's inability to maintain unity on the Reform issue.[16] Following the death of Palmerston in October 1865, Earl Russell (formerly Lord John) had succeeded as Premier, with Gladstone assuming the leadership of the House of Commons, and the new Ministry resolved to introduce a Reform Bill providing for a £7 borough household franchise and a £14 county franchise. This was a very moderate proposal, which would only have enfranchised an extra 400,000 people — mostly the better-off working men — but it was rigorously opposed by a group of some forty Liberal MPs, known as the 'Adullamites', and the Conservatives contrived to vote with them in order to secure the Bill's defeat. When Russell's government resigned in consequence, the prospect arose of a fusion between the Conservatives and moderate Liberal elements, a development long sought by Derby and Disraeli, but in the event this did not take place as it became clear that the Adullamites were unwilling to join a government headed by the existing Conservative leaders. Fusion might have been acceptable under an alternative leader like Derby's son, Lord Stanley, but Derby and Disraeli were not prepared to make the personal sacrifice that this would have required. Instead, Derby proceeded to form a purely Conservative ministry, with Disraeli once again combining the roles of Chancellor of the Exchequer and Leader of the House of Commons, which inevitably had to confront the question of what to do about parliamentary reform.

There were a number of options available to the Conservatives. One was to do nothing, an approach that initially found favour with Disraeli, who thought it might be possible to divert public attention to some issue such as reform of the Admiralty's administration. During the autumn of 1866, on the other hand, ministers inclined more to the view that some attempt ought to be made to settle the reform question, and this was no doubt partly influenced by the popular demonstrations taking place in various parts of the country. Yet there was no great sense of urgency within the Cabinet. As late as January 1867, the intention was to proceed by way of vague resolutions, followed by the appointment of a Royal Commission of inquiry, with a view to legislation in 1868. It was not until 12 February that Disraeli, having gauged the state of opinion in the House of Commons (which was increasingly favourable to immediate action) pledged the government to introduce a bill at once.

However, it remained to be seen what sort of measure the government would propose, given both its precarious position in the Commons and the added complication that opinion within the Cabinet was divided. In an attempt to preserve unity, the government hurriedly put together a plan involving a £6 *rating* franchise for the boroughs (equivalent to about £8 rental) and a £20 county franchise, but it quickly became obvious that a bill drawn along these lines had no chance of being passed. Not only was it bound to be dismissed as inadequate by Gladstone and the Liberals, but, significantly, it failed to satisfy many backbench Conservatives who wished to see their leaders seize the initiative. Derby and Disraeli therefore decided to sacrifice the three Cabinet ministers opposed to a more radical settlement, Lord Carnarvon, Lord Cranborne and General Peel, and put forward an alternative bill, based upon the simple principle of household suffrage for the boroughs together with a £15 county franchise.

The problem for Disraeli was where he was going to find the additional votes in the House of Commons with which to push the Reform Bill through. In practical terms (since Gladstone was unlikely to offer any assistance to his hated rival) the only solution was for Disraeli to bid for the support of those Radical MPs who had wanted a more far-reaching measure than the one offered by their Liberal leaders in 1866. There was certainly considerable scope for concessions to the Radicals, because the Reform Bill of 1867, as it stood when introduced, was deceptively moderate in its provisions. It appeared to be a bold measure in that it adopted household suffrage for the boroughs, which the Radicals had long been demanding, but its operation was severely restricted in practice by the various conditions that were attached. As the bill went through its committee stage in the House of Commons, therefore, Disraeli made a series of modifications designed to satisfy the Radicals and prevent them from supporting Gladstone in any move to wreck the bill. The residence requirement for voters was reduced from two years to one, provision was made for a £10 lodger franchise, and the county franchise was reduced from £15 to £12. Most importantly of all, Disraeli decided to accept the amendment proposed by Grosvenor Hodgkinson which, by abolishing the practice of 'compounding' rents and rates,[17] ensured a vast increase in the number of direct ratepayers who thus became eligible for the vote. It is likely that Disraeli could have secured the rejection of Hodgkinson's amendment, had he wished, but he preferred to allow it to be inserted into the Bill in order to pre-empt any similar action from Gladstone: Disraeli did not mind giving way to demands made by the Radicals, but he had no intention of letting Gladstone dictate the terms of the Bill. By exploiting the divisions within the Liberal ranks, and thus thwarting Gladstone's attempts to create difficulties for the government, Disraeli succeeded in carrying the Reform Bill, even though its provisions were transformed in the process. In its final form, the Bill almost doubled the electorate of England and Wales to nearly two million and gave the working classes a preponderance of votes in many boroughs.

From the Conservatives' point of view, valuable benefits were to be gained from implementing their own Reform Bill. The accompanying redistribution of seats could be kept to the lowest figure that was decently possible: 52 seats were taken from small boroughs (none were completely disfranchised), but 25 of these were given to the English counties. Furthermore, the commissioners responsible for drawing the new constituency boundaries were instructed to separate urban and rural populations as far as possible, so that borough boundaries were expanded to incorporate the urban overspill into the surrounding counties, thereby ensuring that the counties were purified of 'alien' elements. Both these aspects of Parliamentary Reform, redistribution and boundary changes, indicate that the Conservatives were thinking more in terms of strengthening their grip in the counties rather than making significant inroads into Liberal borough territory. Nevertheless, it remains the case that the overriding concern of Derby's third minority government in 1867 was to enhance its credibility in the public mind by producing a comprehensive settlement of a major political issue, and to this end it was necessarily prepared to be flexible as to the details of that settlement.

What is beyond doubt is that Disraeli's personal reputation in the House of Commons was considerably enhanced by the skill he displayed in steering the Reform Bill through. William White, the Radical doorkeeper of the Commons, was particularly struck by the fact that Disraeli had guided the Bill almost single-handedly:

> It has seemed to us, whilst watching the progress of this measure, that the Chancellor of the Exchequer has ruled his Ministry with despotic power. 'You must speak', he seemed to say to one, and he spoke. To others he issued no commands, and they were silent. And more than once — once certainly — with an

appearance of something like contempt, when one of his colleagues had earnestly and eloquently defended a position, Disraeli, with no word of apology to that colleague, rose, and, without noticing the arguments of his 'right hon. friend', opened the gates and conceded the position to the foe. Furthermore, it has been remarked that, whatever may have been done in Cabinet, in the House the leader appeared to consult none of his colleagues.

It is indeed true that Disraeli accepted the Hodgkinson amendment entirely on his own initiative, without seeking the Cabinet's prior approval. In White's judgement, considering the formidable obstacles that Disraeli had had to overcome, it was clear that 'for tact, adroitness, and skill, the man that conquered all these difficulties has no superior, and scarcely an equal, in Parliamentary history.'[18]

Of equal interest to Disraeli's personal triumph in the House of Commons is the way he subsequently presented the Reform Act to the country. In a speech at Edinburgh in October 1867 he repudiated the notion that reform ought to be a Liberal monopoly, and appealed to an 18th century Tory tradition of reform associated with the names of Bolingbroke and Pitt. This was quite in keeping, of course, with the interpretation of history that had informed Disraeli's early writings, such as the 'Vindication of the English Constitution'. A new point was added, however, that when the Whigs passed the Great Reform Act of 1832 they had deprived working men of the right to vote (this was true, to a limited extent), and Disraeli asserted that the Conservatives' aim had been to remedy the sense of grievance arising from this fact. He pointed out, correctly, that the new Reform Act had not created a 'democracy' but was based on the clear principles of household suffrage and personal payment of rates — the latter being a good test of responsible citizenship. In effect, then, Disraeli was maintaining that the Reform Act was the product of a preconceived plan. It was true that it had been necessary for him to gradually 'prepare the mind of the country', and to 'educate' his own party as to the need for a settlement of the reform question, and he claimed to have been engaged in this exercise ever since the earlier abortive Reform Bill of 1859. But he insisted that the Act was a vindication of his party's claim to represent the interests of the whole nation: 'I have always considered that the Tory party was the national party of England...It is formed of all classes, from the highest to the most homely, and it upholds a series of institutions that are...an embodiment of the national requirements and the security of the national rights.'[19]

Herein lay the origins of what was later to be called 'Tory Democracy' — the doctrine which held that the Conservatives' enactment of Parliamentary Reform in 1867 was incontrovertible proof of their confidence in the loyalty and good sense of the masses. This belief may have borne little relation to the truth of how and why the Reform Act was passed, but it generated a mythology of great potency which survived for almost a century. A better guide to Disraeli's attitude towards the working classes is provided by his initial scepticism and suspicion regarding the project to establish a National Union of Conservative and Constitutional Associations. This organisation was conceived as a means of bringing together Conservative working men's associations from all over the country, but its inaugural meeting in London in November 1867 received little encouragement from Disraeli and the Conservative leadership. There was, indeed, considerable unease at the prospect of independent working-class action, even on behalf of a good cause like the Conservative Party. Disraeli's vision of a 'national' party implied that the masses should accept their allotted place within a hierarchical social structure, headed by the traditional ruling elite, and not get ideas into their heads about forming separate organisations.[20]

The Irish Church and the 1868 General Election

In February 1868 ill health finally compelled Derby to resign the Premiership, and at this point there was no serious suggestion of anyone other than Disraeli as the right man to replace him. Disraeli's intense ambition to secure political fame was always clear enough, but even he may not have expected, in the years prior to 1868, that he could achieve the highest office. Derby was only five years his senior and, but for increasingly severe attacks of gout, would certainly have wished to lead the party through the next general election. It is possible that Disraeli was being sincere, therefore, when he maintained that, having served his chief for twenty years, he had assumed that their political careers would end together.[21]

Whatever the truth of this may have been, Disraeli now found himself at the head of a minority administration awaiting the completion of the new electoral registers before a dissolution of Parliament could take place. With the Reform question out of the way, however, Disraeli's government was to be vulnerable to attack from the Liberals on other fronts. The issue that came to dominate parliamentary proceedings, during the session of 1868, was the status of the established (Anglican) Church in Ireland, which had long been condemned by many as anomalous, since it only ministered to about ten per cent of the Irish people. Disraeli's own idea was to try to deflect the criticism of the Church of Ireland by offering concurrent endowment — that is to say, State funding of the Roman Catholic and Presbyterian Churches as well. But any move in this direction was pre-empted by Gladstone, who introduced a series of resolutions in the House of Commons calling for the disestablishment and disendowment of the Irish Church. Gladstone's initiative proved highly effective as a device for reuniting the Liberals, including the Adullamites, and he was therefore easily able to defeat Disraeli's government. Only the threat of an immediate dissolution of Parliament, and an election on the old franchise, deterred Gladstone from following up his victory with a vote of censure and enabled Disraeli and his colleagues to hold on to office for the remainder of the session.

The re-emergence of Church questions at least gave Disraeli a theme for the forthcoming general election, which, as he predicted to the Queen in August, 'will be a great Protestant struggle.'[22] His address to the electors of Buckinghamshire was, indeed, uncompromising in its resistance to disestablishment in Ireland, and Disraeli's stance naturally encouraged Conservatives to exploit anti-Irish feeling in British constituencies by alleging that Gladstone and the Liberals had entered into an unholy alliance with Roman Catholicism. The weakness in Disraeli's address was that it offered nothing more positive with which to attract the newly-enfranchised working classes. Curiously, Disraeli seems to have been misled by his party managers into anticipating significant electoral gains for the Conservatives, who he thought might number as many as 330 in the new Parliament, leaving them only in a very slight minority. When the general election was finally held, in November–December 1868, the grim reality was a heavy Conservative defeat, and Disraeli found himself in a minority of roughly 110. Gains in the English counties had been more than offset by the net loss of thirty-three English borough seats, and in Scotland, where the Conservatives were traditionally weak, a net loss of four left them with just eight seats (out of a possible sixty), while in Ireland a total of forty seats (out of a possible 105) represented a net loss of ten.

As is well known, there was some comfort to be drawn from the victories by Conservative candidates in the City of London, Westminster and Middlesex, the first signs of the phenomenon of business and suburban middle class support for the party in the metropolis, which was to be of immense significance in later elections. Otherwise, the only cause for celebration was provided by an impressive performance in Lancashire, possibly the one area where Disraeli's 'Protestant' campaign had some beneficial effect. The Conservatives achieved a clean sweep of the eight county seats (compared with three out of five in 1865), and won fourteen out of the twenty-five borough seats (including four gains from the Liberals and three of the five new seats provided by redistribution). Lancashire was exceptional for the strength of its working-class Conservatism, which was influenced by paternalistic factory owners like the Hornbys of Blackburn, the power of the 'drink trade', and a strident Protestantism — exemplified by C. E Cawley and W. T. Charley, the triumphant candidates at Salford — arising from the provocative presence of a substantial Irish Catholic immigrant population.[23]

Disraeli broke with constitutional convention in December 1868 by resigning immediately after the election results were complete rather than waiting to be defeated in the new Parliament. This has since become the standard practice for a vanquished Prime Minister, but, as is so often the case, an important constitutional precedent was originally dictated by the tactical considerations of the moment. Disraeli was aware of the divisions within his Cabinet on the Irish Church question, between 'liberals' such as Stanley and Pakington and hard-liners like Gathorne Hardy, and there was no point in exhibiting such differences to the public when the Ministry's days were clearly numbered anyway. On the eve of his sixty-fourth birthday, Disraeli's brief Premiership thus came to an end, and it would have been hard to predict that he would hold office again.

The doldrums

The General Election of 1868 emphatically reaffirmed the Liberals' position as the natural majority party, and the Conservatives' total of some 274 seats marked an electoral retreat almost down to the level of 1857, the year of Palmerston's great victory. Disraeli and his party were restored to their accustomed place on the opposition benches, in circumstances that were particularly unfavourable, since Gladstone could reasonably claim to possess a 'mandate' from the people for his Irish Church policy. A bill to disestablish and disendow the Church of Ireland was duly introduced in 1869, and though Disraeli went through the motions of opposing the measure it was perfectly obvious that he could not hope to stop it. His front-bench colleague, Gathorne Hardy, noted at the time of his speech against the second reading of the Bill, that Disraeli was 'sparkling & brilliant but far from earnest. He gave no reality to his objections', while at the third reading stage Hardy was dismayed by his chief's 'wretched' performance: 'He called out no feeling in his favour.'[24] During the intervening committee stage various amendments were put forward by back-bench Conservatives, but it was clear that Disraeli disapproved of many of them and deprecated the forcing of divisions which merely served to expose the Opposition's weakness.[25] In fact, there was to be a much stronger challenge to the Irish Church Bill from the House of Lords, who made substantial amendments to it, but the government's prestige was so high that it was able to force the peers to give way.

Disraeli's attendance at the House of Commons in 1870 was intermittent owing to ill health, though there was in any case little scope for an effective attack on Gladstone's ministry. For instance, the Conservatives were unwilling to risk opposing the second reading of the Irish Land Bill, which they regarded as an obnoxious but unavoidable necessity. In the case of W. E. Forster's Education Bill, the Opposition even lent the government its support, on the grounds that while the Bill proposed to set up School Boards in areas where the provision of elementary school places was inadequate, it otherwise left the existing Church of England-dominated voluntary system untouched. Forster's plan was vehemently opposed, on the other hand, by many Radicals and Nonconformists on the Liberal backbenches, for precisely the reason that it did nothing to challenge the Church's role as the main provider of elementary education. This early sign of a fissure from within the ranks of the Liberal majority at least offered some hope to the Conservatives for the future, and it was what Disraeli had in mind when Hardy visited him towards the end of May: 'I called on Disraeli, who remains poorly & dreads the East wind. He is desponding but looks forward to Gladstone becoming useless to the Radicals & a disruption. Gives two years or more.'[26] For the time being, nevertheless, it was the publication of a new novel, *Lothair*, in May 1870 (his first since 1847) that attracted more public attention than Disraeli's limited political activity.

During the course of the 1871 session, the Conservatives' prospects brightened appreciably, as Gladstone's ministry encountered serious problems on a number of fronts, and it is important to recognise Disraeli's renewed efforts as Opposition leader at this time. One of the issues causing embarrassment to the government was its helplessness in the face of Russia's decision to position a fleet in the Black Sea, in defiance of the Treaty of Paris (1856). Early in the session, Hardy noted in his diary that Disraeli 'lashed Gladstone into unusual passion', by his remarks on the diplomatic situation. Just a few days later, Disraeli also made a 'cutting and contemptuous speech', criticising the government for its hesitancy in dealing with agrarian crime in Ireland. Admittedly, an attack on Lowe's budget in May was 'not one of [Disraeli's] best feats and... it fell rather flat', but in July, when the government used a Royal Warrant to circumvent the House of Lords' resistance to the Army Regulation Bill, 'Disraeli was more vehement than I ever saw him & was even called to order, not usual with him.' Towards the close of the session, there was also 'some pungent speaking on [Secret] Ballot', as Disraeli condemned the government for its obsession with trying to force this measure through at the expense of more important legislation.[27] Even a Liberal MP had to acknowledge, in his diary, that Disraeli's reputation in the House of Commons was rising again, in sharp contrast to the position of the more impetuous Liberal Premier: 'Gladstone suffers seriously in encounters with Disraeli, who surpasses his rival in calm & premeditation — also, in point.'[28]

Disraeli's greatest concern, from 1871 onwards, was that the government might collapse suddenly, forcing the Conservatives to take office before the time was fully ripe. As Lord Stanley, now the 15th Earl of Derby (his father, the Conservative Premier, had died in October 1869), discovered in a conversation at the beginning of the 1871 session, Disraeli was not at all anxious to turn out the Liberal ministers, 'especially by the help of the ultra-Liberals', but thought that 'it may not be easy to keep them where they are.' He was quite clear that he 'had had enough of being a Minister without a majority: and did not intend to try that position again.' Rather than seizing power prematurely and perhaps only making modest gains at a general election, Disraeli's preference was for compelling the Liberals to soldier on until they were completely discredited, in much the same way that Peel had kept Melbourne and the Whigs on the rack between 1839 and 1841.[29]

In spite of numerous signs of Conservative recovery, there remained grave doubts about the suitability of Disraeli's leadership, and these came to a head at the famous gathering of prominent members of the party at Burghley House in January 1872. Those present included most of the members of the last Conservative Cabinet, together with a few representative backbenchers, and the chief whip, Gerard Noel. Disraeli was not present, of course, nor was the other key individual being discussed, the 15th Earl of Derby. The fullest account of the proceedings is given in Gathorne Hardy's diary:

> At our meeting Cairns boldly broached the subject of Lord Derby's lead & the importance of Disraeli's knowing the general feeling. We all felt that none of his old colleagues could or would undertake such a task as informing him... I expressed my view that Disraeli has been loyal to his friends & that personally I wd. not say I preferred Ld. D. but that it was idle to ignore the general opinion. Noel said that from his own knowledge he cd. say the name of Derby as leader wd. affect 40 or fifty seats. It seemed conceded that the old government could not stand again. What then must follow? Disraeli cd. not combine a new one. Wd. it not be better that he should not try & fail? Why not serve under Derby for wh. there is abundant precedent. [Lowry] Corry s[ai]d he knew that Dis: had no such intention now. Such were some of the incidents of the talk. For my own part I do not look forward with hope to Derby but I cannot but admit that Disraeli has not as far as appears the position in House & Country to enable him to do what the other might.[30]

Only Sir Stafford Northcote and Lord John Manners (the faithful ally from Young England days) appear to have spoken in favour of Disraeli.

The Burghley House meeting can be seen as symptomatic of a loss of nerve on the part of leading Conservatives, who feared that Disraeli's continued *overall* leadership of the party might prove a fatal handicap, preventing them from reaping the full rewards of an increasingly promising political situation. It was felt that the prestige attached to the name of Derby would, in itself, be an enormous asset to the party if the new Earl was willing to take over the reins. There was also the consideration that Derby would have a much better chance of achieving a rapprochement with the rebel Conservative Ministers of 1867, Lords Carnarvon and Salisbury, who were profoundly antagonistic to Disraeli and still unwilling to promise to serve under him in future.[31] Evidently, the prevailing view at Burghley was that the ideal arrangement would involve Disraeli agreeing to defer to Derby's leadership, while remaining in charge of the Conservative party in the House of Commons: in other words, that there should be a Derby-Disraeli 'Mark II' combination. The fatal weakness in this plan, of course, was that there was no reason to suppose that Disraeli would be so obliging as to accept his own demotion, and, in the unlikely event of an ultimatum being delivered to him, the party would have risked turning its leader into a backbench *Frondeur*. In any case, there were those, such as Hardy, who accepted that Disraeli was a liability to the party but also had serious reservations about Derby's capacity for leadership, since his personality was so different from that of his father. Consequently nothing came of the discussions at Burghley, and the idea of finding an alternative leader was largely forgotten as the Conservatives' position continued to improve.

1872: The national party

Disraeli was soon able to reassert his authority as Conservative leader when he made two important appearances on the public platform in 1872 — the first at Manchester's Free Trade Hall, on 3 April, where he spoke for three-and-a-half hours to an audience of 6,000, and later at the Crystal Palace, on 24 June, where he delivered a more concise address.[32] The significance of these speeches lay more in the fact that Disraeli made them at all, and in the nature of the audiences he was addressing, than in their oratorical quality. Disraeli was making a long-deferred visit to Lancashire, in recognition of the Conservatives' electoral success there in 1868, while at the Crystal Palace he was giving a valuable endorsement to the recently-formed National Union of Conservative and Constitutional Associations. In tactical terms, moreover, Disraeli was seizing the opportunity to exploit the growing unpopularity of Gladstone's ministry in order to reinforce the 'Tory' strategy which he had been pursuing for over a decade.

There was little novelty in Disraeli's declaration, at Manchester, that 'the programme of the Conservative party is to maintain the Constitution of the country.' But he proceeded to discuss, at some length, the virtues of the monarchy as a symbol of national unity and a source of political wisdom, the advantages of a powerful House of Lords founded on the basis of 'responsible property... territorial property', and the civilising influence of the Church of England. If Disraeli managed to squeeze some extra political advantage from this approach in 1872, when he had been singing a similar tune for many years, it was because recent events had lent some credence to the idea that these institutions really were in danger. We have already noted that Disraeli had privately expressed concern about the damage being done to the monarchy's reputation by Victoria's shunning of her public responsibilities, and dissatisfaction with the Queen encouraged some to voice republican senti- ments, notably the ambitious young radical MP, Sir Charles Dilke, who made a speech at Newcastle in the autumn of 1871 criticising the cost of the monarchy to the taxpayer. Almost simultaneously, however, there was a wave of public sympathy for the Royal Family occasioned by the serious illness of the Prince of Wales (he nearly died of typhoid fever), and the subsequent thanksgiving service at St. Paul's Cathedral in February 1872 indicated that the monarchy was still capable of tapping into a strong current of popular reverence. The House of Lords meanwhile had allegedly faced a challenge to its constitutional authority from the high-handed conduct of Gladstone's government, which had disregarded the peers' objection to the Army Regulation Bill by resorting to a Royal Warrant in order to achieve its objective. As for the Church of England, Conservatives could point both to the dangerous precedent set by the disestablishment of her sister Church in Ireland, and to the fact that the nonconformist Liberation Society had since renewed its campaign for disestablishment in England. Ominously, 89 MPs voted for Edward Miall's motion in favour of disestablishment during the 1871 session of Parliament. The nonconformist agitation against Forster's Education Act was also indicative of a spirit of malignity towards the Church of England. In various ways, then, it was possible for Disraeli to suggest that either Gladstone's government itself, or else those who supported it on the back benches and in the Country, were harbouring hostile intentions towards ancient and precious national institutions.

Disraeli's treatment of the question of empire, which figured more prominently in his Crystal Palace speech, also involved much repetition of the views expressed ten years earlier in the House of Commons. It was notable, though, for the explicit accusation that the Liberal party had a sinister plan to dispose of Britain's colonies. 'If you look to the history of this country since the advent of Liberalism — forty years ago — you will find that there has been no effort so continuous, so subtle, supported by so much energy, and carried on with so much ability and acumen, as the attempts of Liberalism to effect the disintegration of the Empire of England.' Disraeli rehearsed his standard complaint that the Liberals had granted self-government to the areas of white colonial settlement without providing safeguards for the preservation of links with the mother country, such as a system of imperial tariffs, clear arrangements for defence, or the creation of some form of representative imperial assembly in London. A great opportunity to consolidate the empire had, therefore, regrettably been missed. Disraeli's allegation was that such lamentable neglect was a deliberate part of Liberal policy which aimed to gradually weaken and eventually dissolve the bonds between Britain and her colonies. The reason for this was that the Liberals looked upon the colonies as nothing more than a financial burden, 'totally passing by those moral and political considerations which make nations great, and by the influence of which alone men are distinguished from animals.' Disraeli's grounds for impugning the motives of his political opponents were, it has to be said, rather flimsy, as the Liberals were merely trying to force colonies like New Zealand to bear the cost of their own defence, a policy which Disraeli himself had previously favoured, and which had provoked his notorious outburst about 'millstones'. Nevertheless, Disraeli's comments in 1872 are important for the way they show him endeavouring to add the empire to his list of institutions which the Conservative party was resolved to uphold. Incidentally, his remarks were confined entirely to the existing 'white' colonies, like Australia, New Zealand and Canada, and nowhere in these speeches is it possible to detect any sign that he was looking forward to a new age of imperial expansion.

Liberal mismanagement of foreign policy was discussed at some length at Manchester, two recent episodes providing Disraeli with his main text. According to him, the humiliation inflicted on Britain, when she had been obliged to accept Russia's repudiation of the clauses of the Treaty of Paris excluding the Russian fleet from the Black Sea, was symptomatic of the Liberals' weakness when it came to defending the national interest. Similar problems had arisen in a dispute with the USA over the American claim for damages for the destruction caused by a British-built ship, the *Alabama*, during the American Civil War. It was precisely because Liberal governments were perceived to be weak, in Disraeli's view, that other countries were encouraged to take advantage by behaving unreasonably. He went so far as to assert that if the Conservative Ministry of 1852 had remained in office, the Crimean war (and hence the peace treaty of Paris, with its Black Sea clauses) would never have happened, as the Tsar of Russia would not have been so provocative; and he also maintained that his own government of 1868, if it had been allowed more time, would have satisfactorily resolved the question of arbitration over the *Alabama* claims. It needs to be emphasised that Disraeli was not advocating a 'gunboat' style of diplomacy, but simply stating the importance of 'firmness and decision at the right moment', so as to avoid the embarrassing situations in which Liberal pusillanimity had landed the country. The maintenance of British *prestige*, and therefore power, was the key to everything. Britain's policy towards Europe, he insisted, should be one of 'reserve, but proud reserve.'

In his public speeches of 1872 Disraeli was keen to declare his faith in the political character of the working classes. On both occasions he repeated the claim, originally made at Edinburgh after the passing of the second Reform Act, that the Conservatives had been motivated by a desire to rectify the injustice inflicted on the people by the Whigs, who had deprived working men of the right to vote in 1832. The Conservatives had so acted, Disraeli told his audience at the Crystal Palace, because they were confident that the mass of the people were themselves 'Conservative':

> When I say 'Conservative', I use the word in its purest and loftiest sense. I mean that the people of England, and especially the working classes of England, are proud of belonging to a great Country, and wish to maintain its greatness — that they are proud of belonging to an Imperial Country, and are resolved to maintain, if they can, their empire — that they believe, on the whole, that the greatness and the empire of England are to be attributed to the ancient institutions of the land.

The working classes were 'English to the core' and adhered to 'national principles', and it was for this reason that 'the feeling of the nation is in accordance with the Tory party.' Disraeli never used the term 'Tory Democracy', which only came into vogue after his death, but it is clear that this was what he had in mind.

Disraeli's receptiveness to the merits of 'social' reform was the one aspect of the 'Tory' platform that was comparatively new. Of course, he had had much to say in his Young England days about the need to elevate the condition of the people, but he had shown little interest in social issues after becoming

Conservative leader in the House of Commons. In the autumn of 1871, however, a great deal of press publicity was given to the discussions taking place between leading Conservatives and working men's representatives concerning such matters as housing, hours of work, and technical education.[33] Disraeli himself remained politely aloof from what came to be known as the 'new social alliance', but it at least pointed to the political potential in Conservative action on social reform, which offered a means of appeasing the newly-enfranchised working classes. This seemed all the more desirable in view of recent evidence of a disturbing propensity for strike action on the part of unionised labourers.

No real 'programme' of social reform was unveiled in the Manchester and Crystal Palace speeches, but there was an assertion of the Conservatives' willingness to contemplate a number of measures. At the Crystal Palace there were some promising remarks to the effect that, in seeking to improve the condition of the masses, 'no important step can be gained unless you can effect some reduction of their hours of labour and humanise their toil.' But this statement was immediately qualified by the admission that 'The great problem is to be able to achieve such results without violating those principles of economic truth upon which the prosperity of all States depends.' Disraeli merely observed that the Factory Acts of recent decades had done no harm to British industry. The other area of social policy where Disraeli ventured a few suggestions was sanitary legislation. 'Pure air, pure water, the inspection of unhealthy habitations, the adulteration of food, these and many kindred matters may be legitimately dealt with by the Legislature', he informed the people of Manchester. So far as specific remedies were concerned, Disraeli was extremely cautious, confining himself to a recommendation of his frontbench colleague, Charles Adderley's proposed bill to consolidate the existing legislation on public health (this formed the basis for the Conservatives' Public Health Act of 1875). In this way, it would at least be possible to ascertain 'how much may be done in favour of sanitary improvement by existing provisions.'

One great advantage of concentrating on social reform, in the eyes of Conservative politicians, was that it provided a useful diversion from the 'constitutional' agitations allegedly preferred by the Liberals. The Conservatives were pledging themselves to devote time to the implementation of useful and relatively uncontroversial measures of social improvement, the details of which were left unspecified, as an antidote to their opponents' unhealthy obsession with tampering with the nation's institutions. In other words, a vague commitment to social reform was seen as a necessary part of a political strategy designed to give the country a period of repose from the unsettling effects of Liberal reform: social reform and the preservation of 'Tory' institutions went hand in hand.[34]

To summarise the message in Disraeli's speeches, he was proclaiming the end of a forty-year period in which Liberal or 'cosmopolitan' doctrines had dominated the practice of British government, and welcoming the restoration of the Conservatives to their proper position, true to their glorious 18th century traditions, as the exponents of the 'national' idea. It was to be hoped that the Conservatives would thus rescue the country from the menaces of the Gladstonian regime established in 1868 — 'the first instance in my knowledge of a British Administration being avowedly formed on a principle of violence.' As he explained at Manchester, one had only to look at the sorry state of Ireland, where destructive legislation had merely exacerbated social unrest and prompted the rise of a political movement for Home Rule, to see the consequences of Liberalism:

> Their specific was to despoil Churches and plunder landlords, and what has been the result? Sedition rampant, treason thinly veiled, and whenever a vacancy occurs in the representation a candidate is returned pledged to the disruption of the realm. Her Majesty's...Ministers proceeded in their career like a body of men under the influence of some delirious drug. Not satisfied with the spoliation and anarchy of Ireland, they began to attack every institution and every interest, every class and calling in the Country.

Mercifully, the Liberals were now virtually a spent force, and Disraeli made his famous comparison of the ministerial front bench with 'a range of exhausted volcanoes', though he warned that 'the situation is still dangerous. There are occasional earthquakes, and ever and anon the dark rumbling of the sea.'

Towards victory, 1873–4

Disraeli's public appearances in 1872, momentous as they appear in retrospect, were not followed by any sudden surge of political activity on his part. In fact, the declining health of his wife, Mary Anne, who was dying of cancer, understandably had a distracting effect. When Mary Anne died in December, Disraeli's colleague, Gathorne Hardy, speculated as to the likely consequences of his leader's personal loss, hoping that 'D. may seek occupation in more active political life.' Hardy was invited to Hughenden, the following month, where he discovered to his relief that Disraeli intended to be present at the opening of the parliamentary session: 'it is best that he shd. plunge into the thick of the strife at once.'[35] Disraeli was now in his late sixties, but the prospect of a return to power was at last in sight, and with it the thought that he might vindicate his political course over the past thirty years. The death of his wife — they had no children — can only have made the alternative option, of retirement into private life, less attractive.

Early in the 1873 session, Disraeli was certainly in the 'thick of the strife' once more. Gladstone's ministry focused its legislative energies on Ireland, introducing a bill to restructure the system of university education in that country, which proved to be unacceptable to the Roman Catholic hierarchy (who wanted a university under their own control) as well as to some radical MPs. The Conservative Party joined in the opposition to the bill, though for the quite different reason that they disliked the threat it posed to the status of Trinity College, Dublin, a Protestant institution. This curious combination of Conservatives, Irish Liberals and Radicals was strong enough to narrowly defeat the government, in March, and Gladstone responded by tendering his resignation. It was open to Disraeli to form a government and dissolve Parliament at the earliest practicable moment, but he took the bold decision to decline this opportunity. He repudiated Gladstone's assertion that he was morally obliged to take office, on the grounds that the Conservatives had been part of a chance coalition, hostile to the University Bill, which would not normally act together. The reality was that Disraeli still doubted his party's ability to gain enough seats at a general election to overturn the huge Liberal majority of 1868, and he feared that by agreeing to form a minority government, which would have to make interim financial arrangements before Parliament could be dissolved, he might help his opponents to regroup by giving them a short respite from the problems of office. Disraeli was determined to force the Liberals to struggle on under the burden of ministerial responsibility, until hopefully the processes of party disintegration and growing public disgust were complete. His decision to compel Gladstone and his colleagues to resume their posts caused some dismay amongst Conservative activists, who were eager for power, but it seems to have been considered tactically correct by most on the Opposition front bench.[36] Subsequent events, which left the Liberals floundering for the remainder of the 1873 session with increasing signs of desperation, were to amply justify Disraeli's refusal to take office prematurely.

However, Gladstone was far from finished and, in January 1874, shortly before the new session was due to open, he seized the political initiative by announcing that Parliament would be dissolved immediately and that he was seeking a renewed electoral mandate on the basis of his proposal to abolish the income tax. This thunderbolt undoubtedly alarmed the Conservatives, who could hardly be seen to oppose such a boon to the taxpayer and who had nothing else to offer the electorate by way of a positive programme of reform. Disraeli's Buckinghamshire address was entirely negative, simply promising an end to disruptive organic change and 'harassing' legislation. As the relatively subdued election campaign progressed, the Conservative party managers were predicting gains from the Liberals, but no-one was confident of outright victory.[37] Both sides, in fact, were stunned when it became clear that the Conservatives had secured their first overall parliamentary majority since Peel's in 1841, commanding roughly 350 of the 658 seats in the new House of Commons.

The Conservative Party made net gains of three seats in Wales and twelve in Scotland, but they suffered a net loss of seven in Ireland, where the Home Rule Party had emerged as a powerful political force. A comparison of the election results in 1868 and 1874, given in the following table serves as a reminder that the Conservatives were overwhelmingly the party of England.[38]

Conservative seats in England at two general elections

	1868	1874	(Total seats)
English counties	115	129	(154)
English industrial counties	10	15	(18)
English boroughs (population under 20,000)	52	60	(118)
English agricultural boroughs (population over 20,000)	5	5	(8)
English boroughs (population over 20,000)	34	72	(159)
Total	216	281	(457)

The Conservatives had thus strengthened their already firm grip on the counties while making important gains in the boroughs, especially the most populous ones. Most striking of all was the party's performance in the Metropolis: as late as 1865, not a single Conservative had been elected for a London constituency, but in 1874 three of the four seats in the City itself were captured, along with the second seat in Westminster (following up W. H. Smith's solo victory there in 1868), and fresh gains were made in Marylebone, Chelsea, Greenwich, Southwark and Tower Hamlets. The Conservatives also fared well in the provincial boroughs, notably those in Lancashire, where a net gain of four gave the party control of eighteen out of a possible twenty-five seats in the county.

One explanation that is frequently proffered for the remarkable Conservative triumph in 1874 is that it was largely attributable to the improved state of the party's organisation in the constituencies. This was allegedly due to the efforts of J. E. Gorst, who was appointed as Principal Agent by Disraeli in 1870. Gorst established a new organisational headquarters, Central Office, and closely supervised the efforts of the fledgling National Union, thus ensuring that by 1874 the party was much better prepared for a fight in the critically important large English boroughs.[39] Some scepticism has recently been expressed by historians, however, concerning the significance of Gorst's contribution to the victory. For instance, it has been demonstrated that, contrary to the notion that Gorst had filled what was virtually an organisational vacuum, a good deal of work had been done by the Conservative party managers of the 1850s, Jolliffe, Rose and Spofforth, to lay the foundations for future success. Furthermore, there is the problem of disentangling fact from myth in relation to the 1874 victory. Gorst was a cantankerous individual, who eventually resigned as Principal Agent in 1877 and later pursued a vendetta against the Conservative leadership, aligning himself with Lord Randolph Churchill and the 'Fourth Party' in the 1880s. It therefore suited Gorst to maintain that he had single-handedly won the 1874 general election for an ungrateful party, which never recognised the value of his services. And yet this interpretation ignores the inconvenient fact that Gorst had failed to predict the Conservative landslide at the time of the dissolution. The most that one can say is that Gorst had worked hard to build up the electoral organisation in the larger boroughs, and the Conservatives did relatively well in those constituencies — but one cannot simply assume that *ergo* it was Gorst's machinery that delivered the gains.[40]

There can be little doubt that the key to explaining the Conservatives' electoral breakthrough is to be found in the drift towards Conservatism on the part of the middle classes. Some businessmen had long been Conservative in their politics, of course (including many Lancashire cotton manufacturers), and the increasing willingness of employers to support the party may well have been encouraged by the trade union militancy of the early 1870s, as well as by the general unease about the disruptive tendencies of Gladstonian Liberalism.[41] Frederic Harrison, a radical journalist, thought that in 1874 many small businessmen had also supported the Conservative cause:

> The brewer, the distiller, the soap-boiler, the cotton broker, and the drysalter have strong constitutional principles. The sleek citizens, who pour forth daily from thousands and thousands of smug villas round London, Manchester and Liverpool, read their *Standard* and believe the Country will do very well as it is.[42]

Harrison's reference to 'smug villas' points to an important social phenomenon of the age — the rapid growth of suburbia, visible in all the main towns and cities and in London above all else. Suburbanisation was facilitated by the development of railway communications, which made commuting possible, and it was reinforced by the increasing numbers engaged in 'white collar' occupations. Disraeli has left a poignant note describing how, in the late summer of 1872 when Mary Anne was too ill to make the journey back to Hughenden, they spent their days riding out in a carriage and discovered the new suburban world of London: 'What miles of villas! and of all sorts of architecture! What beautiful Churches! What gorgeous Palaces of Geneva.'[43]

An interesting case study of the way in which London and the Home Counties were swinging decisively behind the Conservatives is provided by East Surrey. Prior to the second Reform Act, this two-member constituency had included business and residential districts south of the river Thames, such as Lambeth, Southwark, Wandsworth, Camberwell and Croydon, but also extended out to Kingston, Richmond and

Reigate. It was dominated by the Liberals, but as early as 1860 there is evidence that East Surrey was being targeted by the Conservatives. Charles Schreiber, a Conservative resident, remarked upon 'the peculiar character of the Constituency': 'no one knows more of his next neighbour than he wd if living in a street in London — & consequently that, throughout the suburban districts, what may be called County influence is entirely wanting.' A registration association had already been set up in 1859, and according to Schreiber it had achieved impressive results in its first year, 'placing 1,000 good Conservative votes upon the Register' and 'removing more than 450 Liberals'.[44] At the 1865 General Election the Conservatives made a concerted effort to wrest the seats from the Liberals, running a local aristocratic candidate, William Brodrick, in harness with a wealthy London merchant, H. W. Peek.[45] Both presented themselves as moderate Conservatives, willing to consider the need for a judicious reform of institutions, but opposed (for example) to any lowering of the franchise that might swamp the middle-class electorate. Their opponents, meanwhile, were content to associate themselves with the prosperity created by Liberal free trade policies. Although the Conservatives' campaign proved unsuccessful, Peek, in third place with 3,333 votes, was less than a hundred behind the second-placed Liberal.[46] As a result of the 1867 Reform Act, East Surrey was divided into two new two-member constituencies and Brodrick and Peek were returned for what was now Mid-Surrey, in 1868, but the Liberals held on in the new Eastern division. However, in the summer of 1871 the Conservatives scored a famous by-election victory in East Surrey, which was interpreted as a public verdict on Gladstone's increasingly beleaguered ministry, whose taxation policies and plans for licensing reform had been particularly unpopular. (The triumphant Conservative candidate was none other than James Watney, of the brewing family.)[47] Finally, in 1874, Watney and another Conservative won decisive victories, by margins of well over 1,000 votes, in a constituency whose registered electorate had increased from 9,986 to 14,977 between 1868 and 1874. Thereafter, East Surrey was safe Conservative territory.

We should be careful, therefore, about ascribing the Conservatives' recovery to a majority position, in the early 1870s, to the wondrous influence of a 'Tory Democracy' invoked by Disraeli. There were, of course, pockets of authentic working-class Conservatism, but these were to become much more significant to the party, electorally, in the years after Disraeli's death. In his 1874 election address, Disraeli offered nothing specifically designed to attract the working men, not even a vague commitment to 'social' reform, the emphasis being placed instead entirely on the need for a period of stability and repose.

If the growing attachment of the middle classes to Conservatism was the most important feature of the 1874 General Election, this raises the awkward question of what Disraeli had really achieved. It is often observed that Peel in the 1840s had attempted to construct a broadly-based 'Conservative' party, representing the interests of all the property-owning classes, and that Disraeli had concentrated his energies into sabotaging this project by asserting the exclusive rights of the landowners. From this perspective, it would seem that the Conservative Party spent a generation in the political wilderness after 1846, only for Disraeli to preside over a process of social assimilation between the upper and middle classes similiar to that he had prevented Peel from achieving.[48] But this is to ignore the extent to which the middle classes had changed since the 1840s, both in terms of the weakening political affinity with Liberalism on the part of employers of labour and tradesmen, and in terms of the expansion of the professions and of 'white collar' occupations like clerks and teachers. All these groups may well have found much to approve of in Disraeli's rhetoric about upholding the ancient institutions of the country and maintaining Britain's imperial strength, and perhaps a little sanitary reform would not necessarily have been considered a bad thing. Disraeli is therefore reasonably entitled to receive credit for having created his own brand of 'Conservatism' by the 1870s, although a later generation would prefer to call it 'Tory Democracy'.

4

PRIME MINISTER, 1874–80

Introduction

Disraeli was in his seventieth year when he formed his second administration. This was certainly an advanced age at which to be entering into untrammelled political power, with a secure parliamentary majority, for the first time, but Disraeli's position was by no means unique. In fact, there was an obvious recent parallel in the career of Lord Palmerston, who had been a year older than Disraeli when he first became Prime Minister and yet remained in office, with one short break, until his death in 1865 at the age of almost eighty-one. Immediately after the 1874 general election, Markham Spofforth, a former assistant party agent, reported to Disraeli a conversation with the editor of the *Morning Post*, Algernon Borthwick (a fervent admirer of Palmerston's), in which Borthwick had expressed the opinion that 'if you [Disraeli] adopt a Palmerstonian policy you will be Prime Minister for life — and that seems to be the general impression.'[1] Presumably what Borthwick had in mind was that Disraeli should combine a cautious approach to domestic questions, avoiding drastic and unsettling reforms, with a firm conduct of foreign policy designed to uphold Britain's interests abroad. Remarks such as Borthwick's are significant evidence of the stunning psychological effect of the Conservatives' unexpected election victory, which seemed to mark a turning-point in British politics: the Liberals' near-monopoly of government had finally been broken, and there was thought to be a real prospect that Disraeli and his party might consolidate their hold on power and retain it for the foreseeable future. Disraeli was indeed to manage a passable imitation of the 'Palmerstonian' style of government between 1874 and 1880, and he enjoyed a fair amount of political success up to 1878, but in the end things went badly wrong for the Conservatives and Disraeli was not to be Prime Minister for life.

Disraeli's government

Compared to the minority Conservative governments of the 1850s and 1860s, Disraeli's ministry of 1874 was much more favourably placed, not only in the obvious sense that it possessed an overall majority in the House of Commons but also in the quality of its executive personnel. Disraeli's ability to put together a respectable ministerial team was a sign of the extent to which the Conservative Party had recovered from the disastrous effects of the schism in 1846. No longer were there to be jibes about a 'Who? Who' ministry, of the kind that had been heard in 1852. Apart from Disraeli and his two veteran colleagues, Lord Malmesbury and Lord John Manners, eight of the nine other Cabinet members appointed in 1874 were men who had first experienced high office in the minority governments of 1866–8. These representatives of a new generation of Conservative leaders included weighty political figures such as Lord Salisbury, Gathorne Hardy, Lord Chancellor Cairns and Sir Stafford Northcote as well as socially prestigious names like the Duke of Richmond and the Earls of Carnarvon and Derby. The one new man in the Cabinet, Richard Assheton Cross, was to prove an outstanding Home Secretary.

Disraeli's greatest achievement, in February 1874, was undoubtedly the reconciliation effected with the two surviving ministers who had resigned over the Reform Bill of 1867, Salisbury (he had then been Lord Cranborne) and Carnarvon.

They had remained estranged from Disraeli's leadership while the Conservative Party was in opposition, and there had even been talk of Salisbury assuming the lead in the House of Lords, which would have been an intolerable arrangement as far as Disraeli was concerned. However, Disraeli's position was enormously strengthened by the scale of the election victory in 1874, and this left Salisbury and Carnarvon with little alternative but to come to terms with the new Prime Minister if they were not to condemn themselves to the political wilderness. Their adhesion to the government ensured that Disraeli was able to assemble his Cabinet from the strongest material available.

The composition of Disraeli's government provides a clear indication of the social balance of power within the Conservative Party and of the Premier's own social bias in the matter of appointments. Of the twelve Cabinet members, one half were peers, and of the commoners, one was the son of a duke and four (including Disraeli) were landowners. Disraeli was always disdainful of 'middle class' men, disliking as he did their parvenu social manners, and he considered them unsuited for the task of government. It was only on the prompting of Derby that he admitted Cross to the Cabinet as the one exception to the aristocratic and landed rule. Even Cross was from an old Lancastrian banking family (he had been educated at Rugby and Cambridge) but his appointment was seen as an important gesture to Lancashire Conservatism. The social exclusivity which generally characterised Disraeli's Cabinet selections was equally apparent in the junior ranks of the government, where berths were found for the likes of Lord Henry Lennox, Lord George Hamilton, the Earl of Pembroke, Frederick Stanley (Derby's brother), George Bentinck and Sir Michael Hicks Beach. These appointments had a mixed success, though Hamilton, Stanley and Hicks Beach were to achieve Cabinet status later on. The only concessions made to 'middle class' feeling within the Conservative Party came with the inclusion of W. H. Smith, the bookstall magnate, as a Junior Lord of the Treasury and Lord Sandon (actually the eldest son of the Earl of Harrowby, but, as an MP for Liverpool, considered to be representative of the commercial interest) as Vice-President of the Council, responsible for education. Both were later promoted to Disraeli's Cabinet and in so doing became the only borough MPs to sit in it. Smith and Sandon were certainly important exceptions to Disraeli's general rule, but it remains the case that the government contained an overwhelming preponderance of men from aristocratic and landed backgrounds, testifying to the Premier's desire to demonstrate the continued capacity for leadership in the traditional ruling elite. Junior ministerial places could be found for such men as Sir Massey Lopes, Sir Henry Selwin-Ibbetson, George Sclater-Booth and Clare Sewell Read — thus confirming in the eyes of backbench Conservatives that theirs was still the party of the landed interest — but none of the businessmen returned for borough constituencies, like W. R. Callendar of Manchester or Edward Bates of Plymouth, seem to have been considered for office. It is a telling sign of the Conservative Party's priorities in 1874 that the President and Vice-President of the Board of Trade were Sir Charles Adderley and George Bentinck, respectively a landowner and the son of a duke, and that Adderley was not even granted Cabinet status.[2]

After a generation of almost permanent exclusion from office, the Conservatives' appetite for patronage was ravenous, and Disraeli always took a robust view of the 'natural' connection between the dispensing of offices and honours, on the one hand, and considerations of party advantage on the other.[3] Patronage was considered to be a vital resource for promoting Conservative cohesion within Parliament and for rewarding faithful supporters outside. Despite the civil service reforms, enacted by Gladstone's Ministry, there were still some positions that could be filled by nomination rather than examination, and in the case of appointments to the Inland Revenue, for example, Disraeli was determined to treat these as 'political prizes'. India and other colonies, meantime, provided a rich supply of employment in offices great and small, where the principle of objective merit did not apply. Many appointments in the Church of England were also in the government's hands, ranging from the selection of archbishops, bishops and deans down to the Lord Chancellor's gift of certain parish livings. In the religious sphere, the fact that bishops and clergymen often wielded considerable electoral influence by virtue of their office was always an important consideration for the government, quite apart from such matters as doctrinal affiliation. Disraeli and his colleagues seem to have felt little inhibition about using the patronage nexus at their disposal to take care of their own relatives, and we thus find Disraeli awarding a commissionership in the Inland Revenue to Northcote's son, Northcote securing a place in the Department of Woods and Forests for Gathorne Hardy's son, and Cross appointing Cairns's nephew as a sub-inspector of factories.

Honours were a particularly useful way of rewarding those who had served the Conservative Party well. During the course of Disraeli's second Ministry, he appointed thirty-nine Lord Lieutenants of counties — an important mark of distinction for members of the aristocracy — and these were judged strictly on party criteria. Interestingly, Disraeli was less lavish than Gladstone when it came to creating new peers, which no doubt reflected a jealous wish to preserve the exclusive character of the House of Lords. He once described the necessary qualifications for a peerage as 'vast possessions, noble lineage, and devotion to the Conservative Party.'[4] However, a lesser hereditary honour was also available in the form of baronetcies, and while many of these were reserved for MPs representing counties, Disraeli was prepared to award a few titles to businessmen sitting for boroughs, such as Callendar, Bates and Greenall.

Turning to Disraeli's management of his Cabinet colleagues, it appears that he was generally content to keep the team together on a loose rein, refraining (except in the case of the Foreign Office) from interference in the work of the various departments and leaving policy initiatives to the relevant ministers. This relaxed style of leadership was potentially hazardous, and there were some retrospective criticisms, notably from Salisbury, of Disraeli's failure to properly supervise the work of certain ministers like the successive Colonial Secretaries, Carnarvon and Hicks Beach.[5] Nevertheless, Disraeli's approach may well have contributed to the harmonious atmosphere within the Cabinet which prevailed for most of the Conservatives' time in office. Gathorne Hardy commented in his diary on several occasions about false rumours of ministerial dissensions and was much amused at their inaccuracy. In April 1876, for instance, he wrote that, contrary to 'Newspaper accounts of our disagreements', there was in fact 'constant concord' at Cabinet meetings. Similarly, in May 1877 he recorded that 'Our Cabinet yesterday was very unanimous & cordial & we could only laugh at the reports of dissension & disunion.'[6] The only period in which Cabinet proceedings did become stormy was in late 1877 and early 1878, when disputes over the Eastern Question, and the possibility that Britain might be drawn into war with Russia, culminated in the resignations of Carnarvon and Derby.[7] Once the air had been cleared, however, harmony seems to have been restored, and Lord Sandon, a new recruit in May 1878, recorded how he was 'generally much struck by the evident unanimity of the Cabinet — by their business-like manner — and thorough knowledge of their own Departments — and I felt that one could hardly be associated with a more high minded and efficient body of men.'[8]

Disraeli once again benefited, as he had in 1868, from a good relationship with the Queen, which became increasingly intimate as time went on. Victoria had never been on cordial terms with Gladstone and, after the experience of dealing with him as Prime Minister for over five years, her feelings had developed into something approaching strong dislike of what she considered to be his dangerously unpredictable, radical tendencies. Disraeli took advantage of his sovereign's growing disposition towards Conservatism, establishing a close personal rapport through outrageous flattery and a careful attention to the Queen's convenience. At times Disraeli's letters to her took on an almost conspiratorial tone, and he certainly played up to her sense of what was her due prerogative in a way that was constitutionally dubious. The end result was that, by the time of Disraeli's resignation in April 1880, Victoria had become so partisan in her attitudes that she *hated* Gladstone for having dared to attack her beloved First Minister, and literally described him as a madman.[9]

In the House of Commons, Disraeli's position was strengthened by the fact that the Opposition was in disarray. During the 1874 session, the Liberals were left leaderless as Gladstone refused to commit himself to the service of his party, feeling that he had been betrayed by its unfaithful conduct towards his late administration. Furthermore, the 1874 General Election had seen the emergence of an independent Home Rule party in Ireland, consisting almost entirely of disillusioned Liberals, which was over fifty strong in the new Parliament and disinclined to cooperate with the Opposition. For various reasons, then, Disraeli's government was in an even more impregnable position than its majority on paper suggested. These favourable circumstances help to explain how he was able to get away with supporting the most controversial item of legislation introduced in 1874, the Public Worship Regulation Bill.[10] This measure was brought forward privately by the Archbishop of Canterbury and was designed to establish a clear procedure whereby clergymen guilty of using ritualistic practices could be disciplined by their bishops. It was yet another manifestation of the Victorians' obsessive fear that their national Church was being contaminated by Catholic influences. While the Bill was being debated in the House of Lords, the government officially adopted a neutral stance, partly in deference to the feelings of High Church colleagues like Salisbury and Carnarvon, who disliked the idea of a witch hunt against ritualists. However, during the Bill's passage through the Commons, Gladstone emerged from his semi-retirement and tried to give a lead, by condemning the measure, a move that encouraged Disraeli to abandon his neutrality and make a speech aligning himself with 'Protestant' feeling in the House and in the country. He defended the Public Worship Regulation Bill on the grounds that it was needed to suppress what he called the 'mass in masquerade'. With the majority of Liberal MPs also supporting the Bill, Gladstone was forced into an embarrassing retreat, and it was eventually carried without a division. The Speaker of the House of Commons, Henry Brand, summing up the 1874 session in his diary, had little doubt that 'Disraeli will have gathered popularity for his Govt by the course he has taken', and judged that his handling of the issue had shown that 'in truth he is in every way a very skilful leader of the H of C.'[11]

If anything, the prospects for Disraeli and his government looked more promising still in the early months of 1875. Gladstone formally resigned as leader of the Liberal Party in January, and though a successor was eventually agreed to in the shape of the Whig, Lord Hartington, his ability to command the united support of Opposition MPs in the division lobby was extremely doubtful. Describing the parliamentary situation in March 1875, Henry Lucy, one of the outstanding journalists of the late Victorian era, found that Disraeli was able to do pretty much what he pleased. 'Disraeli came into power as the avenger of the outraged principle of rest', and in Lucy's view the Prime Minister was the perfect leader to suit the temper of the times, as he 'has the patience which makes possible a masterly inactivity', helpfully combined with a touch of humour. The comparison with his Liberal predecessors was instructive:

> Never, even in the best days of Palmerston, has the House been so docile under management as during the current session. In the day of his power, Gladstone ruled the House, but did not lead it... [but] Disraeli never domineers over the House. On the contrary, he rather goes out of his way to assert that the House is arbitrator of its own acts, and that he is its very humble servant.

Disraeli's willingness to make concessions to minority opinion was particularly important, as it helped to ensure that sittings of the House were shorter, yet more productive, than had been the case in Gladstone's time. Lucy even thought that Disraeli had managed to transmit his own 'conciliatory disposition' to most of his frontbench colleagues — 'In this also he has educated his party.'[12]

In view of Henry Lucy's ability to appreciate Disraeli's merits as a parliamentary leader, it is all the more remarkable to find the same journalist, at the end of the 1875 session, writing of 'Disraeli's personal failure' as the 'striking phenomenon' of the year.[13] Quite suddenly, it seems, Disraeli lost his grip on the House of Commons, badly managing some tricky issues involving individual Members of Parliament and even displaying a violent loss of temper, on one occasion, against an old foe, Robert Lowe. No doubt Disraeli's deteriorating health was at the root of the problem, for he was suffering from repeated attacks of gout, asthma and bronchitis. One evening, late in June 1875, Lucy recorded that Disraeli was 'in a condition almost unrecognisable.' He had had to announce to the Commons that he had made a procedural blunder on a certain matter, and when he followed this statement with a long-anticipated speech on the Agricultural Holdings Bill, 'the attempt was a lamentable failure, and the House observed with sorrow the feeble grasp, the wandering vision, and the irrelevant argument of its former master. Disraeli felt it too, as, broken in spirit and wearied in body, he sat down amid the cheerless silence of the inattentive House.'[14] Disraeli's declining parliamentary reputation continued to be the subject of gossip in political circles into the 1876 session, and Lucy felt obliged to remark that:

> It would be a sad ending to a brilliant career to see Disraeli openly discredited in the assembly of which he has for thirty years been a chief ornament... of late, in increasing measure, he is losing his airy grace of manner, just sufficiently spiced with audacity, and his felicitousness of phrase, always admirably spiced with personality. When these are gone, the House, looking at what is left, finds that it is not much and is not at all desirable.

He appeared to have lost his happy touch when it came to making jokes, and these now came across merely as rudeness; while he was painfully ineffective in dealing with questions.[15]

At the end of the 1876 session, Disraeli wisely retired from the leadership of the House of Commons and went to the

Upper House as the Earl of Beaconsfield. (For the sake of simplicity, I shall continue to refer to him as Disraeli.) Speaker Brand's reaction to Disraeli's departure was one of surprise, but only in the sense that he had delayed for so long in taking the decision to relinquish a post for which 'he has been for some years physically unequal.'[16] As his successor in the Commons Disraeli chose the Chancellor of the Exchequer, Northcote, a conciliatory figure, in preference to the more combative (but also hot-tempered) Gathorne Hardy, who subsequently requested a peerage. In retrospect, Northcote was to prove a bad appointment, as he lacked the requisite firmness in dealing with the House of Commons, when circumstances turned against the Conservatives in the last years of the decade. It may be doubted, however, that any alternative leader would have been able to significantly alter the government's eventual fate. But before we consider why things went so disastrously wrong for Disraeli and the Conservatives, it is appropriate to look at their constructive achievements.

Social reform

It is a commonplace observation that, despite the attention given to social reform in Disraeli's famous public speeches of 1872, the Conservatives had no clearly worked-out legislative programme ready for implementation when they took office in 1874.[17] This fact should be less surprising than it is often made to seem. Gladstone, after all, had plunged the country into a sudden and completely unexpected general election contest in January 1874, and the Conservatives had been far from confident of success. In any case, it was not the accepted practice at this time for party leaders to issue detailed manifestos, listing their plans of action: if anything at all was specified, the emphasis tended to be placed on a single issue, like the income tax, while broad statements of intent were added in the hope of setting a certain tone to the election campaign. Disraeli achieved this through his assurances that the Conservatives would give the country a rest from harassing legislation. Furthermore, Disraeli was not the sort of politician who interested himself in the minute details of legislation, and only a totally inexperienced Minister like R. A. Cross (a man hitherto outside the Conservative inner circle), whose memoirs are often quoted by historians, could have seriously expected his leader's mind to be full of matured policies.[18]

Unprepared for power as it was, the few measures introduced by the new adminstration in the 1874 session were determined largely by the desire to pay off certain election debts. The licensed victuallers were a powerful pressure group, who had assisted the Conservative cause because of their dislike of the Gladstone ministry's legislation affecting the drink trade, and the Intoxicating Liquors Bill therefore obligingly relaxed the rules on public house opening hours imposed by the Liberals in 1872. Another issue on which there was strong pressure for the government to act, coming especially from Lancashire MPs, was the demand for a statutory maximum nine-hour working day in factories. The ministerial approach to this problem was to bring in a bill imposing a maximum $56\frac{1}{2}$ hour week (a six-day working week was still the norm) for women and children, a form of State intervention that could easily be justified on the grounds that women and children were not free agents, capable of negotiating for themselves, and were therefore in need of legislative protection. In practice, though, such a measure was bound to have an indirect effect upon the working hours of men, particularly in the textile industry where women and children made up a majority of the workforce. Cross's Factory Bill thus went a long way towards satisfying the demand for a nine-hour day, but without statutorily regulating the conditions of work applying to men, as this would have been considered by many as an unacceptable form of State interference. This bill has been described, by the authority on the Conservatives' social reforms as 'perhaps the only really paternalist...measure which the Ministry was to pass.'[19]

Certainly, there was to be no question of the Conservatives embarking upon a systematic exercise in paternalistic social reform, inspired by the sort of 'One Nation' principles that Disraeli had laid down in his Young England days. Disraeli may still occasionally have used language reminiscent of his earlier views — for instance, his assertion in 1872 that 'the condition of the people' was the issue of prime importance for politicians — but in reality his government's response to such matters was influenced by the prevailing doctrines of political economy. A generation of Conservative administrators had grown up — men like Northcote and Cross, who were imbued with the teachings of mid-Victorian laissez-faire Liberalism — and there is little to suggest that Disraeli dissented from such thinking. Even if he had, his apathy, when it came to the detailed work of drafting legislation, would have meant that he was unlikely to be able to challenge his colleagues' views effectively. In these circumstances, a cautious, piecemeal approach to the extension of the State's responsibilities was only to be expected from Disraeli's government. There were also inevitably going to be serious financial constraints, limiting the Conservatives' scope for constructive action. For instance, Northcote, the Chancellor of the Exchequer, had inherited a healthy budget surplus from the Liberals in 1874, and he was resolved to devote the bulk of the available financial resources to cutting taxes. This he did in his first Budget by taking 1d. off the income tax (he later took another 1d. off, reducing the rate to a crippling 2d. in the pound), abolishing the duty on sugar altogether (a boon to all classes in society), and, significantly, relieving some of the burden on ratepayers by providing £1.25 million to offset the cost of lunatic asylums and the police.

Nevertheless, it is right to acknowledge the impressive legislative record of the Conservatives in the session of 1875, and to a lesser extent in 1876, which shows that limited intervention by the State was accepted as expedient when the purpose was to encourage individual responsibility. Northcote's Friendly Societies Bill (1875) was prompted by fears about the financial stability of many of these institutions, which provided insurance cover for millions of people, but the Chancellor of the Exchequer's solution was simply to compel the societies to publish more information about themselves, in the belief that this would help individual members of the public to make an informed choice as to the society to which they could most safely entrust their money. The suggestion that the government should go further and provide financial guarantees to cover the possible collapse of any of the societies was emphatically ruled out by Northcote. In the case of the Merchant Shipping Bills of 1875 and 1876, the government sought to deal with the scandal of unsafe or overloaded vessels sent out to sea by unscrupulous owners, but the provisions for increased powers of inspection by the Board of Trade and for load lines on ships to be fixed by the *owners* themselves failed to satisfy the demands of the Radical MP, Samuel Plimsoll, for compulsory inspection and an official load line. The heated public agitation surrounding this issue did a great deal of damage to the government's reputation, as well as revealing the incapacity of the Minister involved, Adderley, who took the view that governments 'did not search every honest man in order to catch offenders', and that it should 'leave all men to manage their own affairs, under the necessary conditions of responsibility to others for the consequence of any careless-ness or neglect on their part.'[20] Lord Sandon's Education Bill (1876) endeavoured to encourage children's attendance at elementary schools, but Sandon's personal preference for compulsion went too far for many backbench Conservatives and he therefore had to pursue his objectives by indirect means — for instance, requiring that children between the ages of ten and fourteen should not be employed unless they had a certificate of school attendance, or one of academic attainment. In this way, it was intended that parents should see that it was in their own interests to have their children educated. Incidentally, Sandon's Bill had a partisan motive behind it, in that he was seeking to promote school attendance as a means of propping up the voluntary Church of England schools, especially in rural areas.

Much of the government's legislation was of the 'permissive' kind, designed to facilitate, but not compel, activity at the local level. The best example is Cross's Artisans' and

Labourers' Dwellings Improvement Bill (1875), which provided that, in 87 specified towns and cities, local authorities could demolish slum properties if the Medical Officer of Health certified them as insanitary. Local authorities were empowered to acquire the offending properties by compulsory purchase, and loans were available from the Public Works Loans Commissioners to assist with the cost. However, the measure was entirely permissive, in the sense that there was no obligation on local authorities to act unless they wished to, and by the end of the decade only ten authorities had made use of the powers available to them. Another revealing restriction in the Bill was that, while local authorities were given the right to clear away slums, the provision of new housing was still to be a matter for private enterprise. Cross was therefore able to argue that his Bill did not infringe the laws of political economy, as the State was merely acting to prevent the human waste caused by disease in slum areas, and that forcing slum landlords to sell would make building land available and thus stimulate private enterprise.[21] Other specimens of Conservative permissive legislation included the Sale of Food and Drugs Bill (1875), which contained comprehensive provisions against the practice of adulteration but did not compel local authorities to employ the analysts needed to enforce the law; and the Pollution of Rivers Bill (1876), which outlawed pollution by 'noxious fluids' but left it to County Court judges to define these, and in any case allowed the culprits ample time to clean up their operations before they could be punished. Both these measures were the work of the President of the Local Government Board, George Sclater-Booth. A final illustration is provided by the Agricultural Holdings Bill (1875), piloted by Clare Sewell Read, which established a legal framework to enable tenant farmers to claim compensation from landlords for unexhausted improvements made to the holding they were vacating. This was a purely voluntary measure that could only be enforced if the landlord and tenant had agreed to adopt it as part of their contract.

In order to assess the contribution made by the Conservatives in the field of social reform, it has to be appreciated that most of their Bills were really the product of the administrative machine and might just as easily have been implemented by another government. Thus, the legislation covering merchant shipping, friendly societies, public health and pollution all followed inquiries by Royal Commissions, while the Artisans' Dwellings Bill was influenced by pressure from the London Medical Officer of Health and the Charity Organisation Society. Nor should we exaggerate what these measures achieved in practice: the Merchant Shipping, Friendly Societies and Pollution Bills proved to be ineffective, and though some slum clearances took place under the auspices of the Artisans' Dwellings Bill, the government's budgetary problems towards the close of the decade meant that the loans to local authorities dried up. As for Sclater-Booth's Public Health Bill of 1875, this did provide a durable settlement in this area of policy, but it did so by consolidating and enforcing the existing sanitary laws without creating any new powers for local authorities.

We have already noted that Disraeli took little personal interest in his government's social legislation and left the initiative almost entirely to colleagues, like Cross, who were committed to an active policy in the belief that the State had the power to do good in certain restricted areas. In Cabinet, Disraeli was apt to doze off when social policy was being discussed.[22] It is, nevertheless, fair to say that Disraeli provided some impetus for a constructive Conservative policy through his general assertions of the party's intention to devote its energies to social legislation, even if he never specified what that legislation was going to be. Such was the message of his speeches in 1872, and it was reiterated at the Mansion House dinner in July 1874, where he pledged his new government to take positive action in the next parliamentary session (which indeed yielded much of the legislative fruits of Conservative rule). Disraeli was therefore faithful to his stated view that useful, non-contentious social reform measures were an appropriate form of action for the Conservatives as an antidote to the Liberal Party's obsession with attacking national institutions like the Church and the House of Lords.[23]

The one area in which Conservative policy had a potentially wider political significance was the reform of the laws regulating trade unions. A sharp rise in the number of industrial disputes in the early 1870s had made this an issue of pressing importance. Cross decided to go further than the recommendations of a recent Royal Commission and, with the crucial support of Disraeli, overcame opposition in the Cabinet to conceding the whole of the demands made by the Trades Union Congress. The Conspiracy and Protection of Property Bill altered the law of conspiracy, so that it no longer applied to trade union activities; the Criminal Law Amendment Act was repealed, making peaceful picketing lawful; and the Employers and Workmen Bill removed the operation of the criminal law from the contractual relations between employers and employees (except in the gas and water industries), meaning that it was no longer possible for workmen to be prosecuted for breach of contract. These measures, all carried in 1875, were presented by Cross as perfectly consonant with the principles of political economy, since they were doing no more than putting workmen on an equal legal footing with their employers. At a relatively late stage in the process, Disraeli began to enthuse about his Home Secretary's policy, believing that it would end the conflict between capital and labour and 'gain and retain for the Tories the lasting affection of the working classes.'[24] Sadly for Disraeli's hopes, the publicly-expressed gratitude of organised labour for the Conservative reforms did not translate into any weakening of its traditional allegiance to the Liberal party, though it is of course true that organised labour represented only a very small proportion of the working classes. By 1880, however, it is unlikely that many working men were influenced in their voting behaviour by recollections of a Conservative programme of social reforms which had receded into the distant past.

Increasingly, from 1876 onwards, the Conservatives became preoccupied with other problems, notably in the fields of imperial and foreign policy. It is hard to accept the view that these distractions from social reform had anything to do with the Conservatives becoming a more 'bourgeois' party, hostile to State interventionism: a simpler explanation is that most late-Victorian politicians attached a far lower priority to social reform than some modern historians, and that ameliorative legislation was therefore only given serious attention in times of political tranquility. In any case, bearing in mind the Conservatives' respectable record in the sessions of 1874–6, it is difficult to understand how the party could suddenly have come under the influence of 'bourgeois' ideology.[25] The fact remains, however, that the Conservatives were diverted from social reform by other issues, and it is to these that we must now turn our attention.

Imperialism

It was seen in Chapter 3 that while Disraeli had in the past publicly asserted the importance of Britain's empire, notably in the Crystal Palace speech of June 1872, he was not the prophet of a new age of imperial expansion. His remarks had been essentially backward-looking, condemning the Liberals for their alleged neglect of the empire, and he was referring only to the areas of white colonial settlement. The record of his second ministry confirms the absence of any great imperial vision on Disraeli's part and shows that he responded almost entirely to the initiatives of others.

Disraeli's lack of interest in imperial policy is illustrated by his attitude towards one of those minor territorial acquisitions which all Victorian governments found themselves making from time to time: the Fiji Islands (1874). The Prime Minister was content to leave this matter to the discretion of his Colonial Secretary, Carnarvon, who was merely following a policy already laid down by his Liberal predecessor, Lord Kimberley. Naturally, this did not prevent Disraeli from hailing the annexation of Fiji, after the event, as proof of the Conservatives' commitment to strengthening the empire.[26] More significantly, in view of his statements in 1872, Disraeli showed no desire to take any steps towards consolidating Britain's ties with her 'white' colonies. This is demonstrated by the way he allowed Carnarvon to take the initiative in Southern Africa, where the Colonial Secretary was keen to establish a federal structure embracing British and Dutch settlements, along the lines of the Canadian constitution of 1867, as the best means of maintaining British authority in an area of vital strategic importance. Disraeli's well-known reaction to Carnarvon's scheme was to declare that 'In all these affairs I must trust to you...Do what you think wisest.'[27] Carnarvon thought it wisest to exploit the vulnerability of the Dutch settlers in the Transvaal to attack from native tribes, putting pressure on them to accept British annexation of their state (1877). This was meant to be a stepping stone towards the creation of a South African Federation within the British Empire. The consequences of Carnarvon's policy only became fully apparent after his resignation, but Disraeli's government found itself saddled with the political responsibility for a war against the Zulus to protect the Transvaal, provoked by the over-zealous Sir Bartle Frere, the British High Commissioner in South Africa, whom Carnarvon had appointed. Worse still, the war went disastrously wrong in the early stages, with a British detachment of some 1,200 men being massacred at Isandhlwana in January 1879. It was to require additional troops, and several months, before the Zulus were defeated, and even this could not repair the damage done to the government's standing in the eyes of British public opinion. Disraeli was certainly unfortunate that he and his colleagues came to be identified with an aggressive policy in South Africa which was not what they had intended and which arose from the actions of an imperial administrator who had disobeyed orders from London.

Britain's involvement in the Suez Canal region provides a truer picture of the Disraelian approach to imperial affairs.[28] In November 1875, Disraeli achieved a remarkable political coup when he succeeded in purchasing, for £4 million, the Khedive of Egypt's 44 per cent stake in the Suez Canal Company. This move received a great deal of favourable publicity at home, seeming to confirm the government's determination to protect British interests in this vital waterway. Above all, the shares purchase was regarded as an effective way of countering French influence in the area — which was considerable, since it was the French who had constructed the canal — and of gaining greater political leverage over the Khedive. However, it would be wrong to suppose, as some contemporaries did, that Disraeli's action was part of a carefully prepared plan intended to culminate in the annexation of Egypt itself. Disraeli showed no interest in such an imperial adventure, being anxious merely to ensure that Britain was able to compete with France in exercising influence over a Khevidal regime which was heading towards financial collapse. By 1879, indeed, a reasonably satisfactory system of dual financial control over Egypt by Britain and France had been established. Ironically, it was left to Gladstone, the most trenchant critic of everything Disraelian, to shoulder the responsibility for Britain's occupation of Egypt in 1882, a year after Disraeli's death.

The underlying consideration for British policy in the Near East, of course, was the need to protect the fastest trading route to India, her most valuable imperial possession. All governments were naturally anxious to maintain control over India, where the fragility of Britain's position had been exposed by the mutiny of 1857, and Ministers were haunted by the fear that Russian expansion into central Asia might eventually lead to a challenge for supremacy in India. The Royal Titles Act of 1876, which made Queen Victoria Empress of India, was thus intended to be a symbolic statement of British power, establishing the Queen as the imperial equal of the Tsar of Russia. Interestingly enough, the impetus for this constitutional change came from the Queen herself rather than the Prime Minister, although it seemed to be stamped with the hallmark of a grand Disraelian imperial gesture.[29] Unhappily for the government, its subsequent policy in India became the victim of another hijacking by an ambitious imperial administrator, this time the Viceroy, Lord Lytton. It was Lytton, acting on his own initiative and also defying orders from London, who precipitated a war against Afghanistan in

December 1878 in an attempt to eliminate Russian influence in that country, which was deemed to pose a threat to the security of India's northwest frontier. Disraeli had not sought this conflict, but his careless remarks about the absence of a 'scientific frontier' for India, in a speech at the Guildhall in November encouraged the perception that the Afghan war was the deliberate outcome of a sinister imperial plan. Initally, Lytton's policy met with success, and the Amir of Afghanistan was obliged to accept the presence of a British mission in Kabul, led by General Cavagnari. However, the reputation of Disraeli's government suffered another devasting blow (following the one inflicted by the Zulus) when Cavagnari's mission was massacred in September 1879. This necessitated the despatch of another military force into Afghanistan, which faced a severe struggle before victory was secured.

In reality, therefore, Disraeli's imperial vision had consisted of little more than flamboyant gestures, designed to impress public opinion. His presentation of the annexation of Fiji, the purchase of the Suez Canal shares and the Royal Titles Act all testified to Disraeli's awareness of the value of imagination in politics. Unluckily for the Conservatives, individuals and events largely beyond the government's control — and it has to be remembered that communications between Britain and her colonies were very slow, a message sent from London taking some weeks to reach its destination — served to create a false impression that Disraeli was executing a pre-conceived plan for imperial expansion in various parts of the globe. And although it was ill-founded, the belief that Disraeli did have grand imperial designs, and that these had resulted in botched and expensive military campaigns, was what shaped the attitudes of a British public increasingly disenchanted with his government by the end of the 1870s.

Jingoism

Throughout his political career, Disraeli can be found insisting that it was the duty of governments to uphold the empire of England. Appropriately enough, this was the central message of his last speech in the House of Commons, on 11 August 1876.[30] But when he spoke in such terms, Disraeli was usually not referring simply to the defence of the colonies but to the wider issue of maintaining Britain's prestige in the eyes of the rest of the world, of which her imperial possessions were only one part.[31] Disraeli was disturbed by the fact that since the mid-1860s Britain had become increasingly isolated and powerless in its relations with the European Powers. In particular, he resented the way that the recently consolidated German Empire, under the leadership of Bismarck, had established itself as the dominant force in European diplomacy through its manipulation of the Dreikaiserbund (Three Emperors' League) formed with Russia and Austria in 1873. Foreign policy was to be the one area of government where Disraeli consistently played an active part, because of his determination to reverse the isolationist trend and, by boldly asserting Britain's interests abroad, to claim for the Conservative Party the 'Palmerstonian' mantle.

The consequences of Disraeli's preference for an interventionist foreign policy became clear in 1876, when the Eastern Question returned to the forefront of diplomatic attention.[32] For many decades, the Turkish (or Ottoman) Empire, which extended into a large area of south-eastern Europe, had been crumbling, and in the mid-1870s nationalist uprisings in several of her Balkan provinces posed a serious challenge to Turkish authority. The Dreikaiserbund responded to this situation by issuing the so-called Berlin memorandum of May 1876, calling on the Turks to institute reforms in the disturbed provinces, and hinting at collective action by the Powers to enforce change if it was not forthcoming voluntarily. Having settled amongst themselves the contents of the memorandum, the Dreikaiserbund then passed it on to the British, French and Italian governments for their endorsement. Disraeli, however, refused to accept the document on the grounds that Britain had not been consulted in advance. A British fleet was meanwhile sent to Besika Bay, on the mouth of the Dardanelles, to serve as a warning that

Britain's views could not be ignored. Disraeli was not prepared to see Britain treated as a secondary power in Europe and he had therefore gratefully seized the chance to publicly snub the Dreikaiserbund. It appears that, at this early stage, he was not primarily motivated by a concern for the integrity of the Turkish Empire.

The decision to reject the Berlin memorandum seemed popular enough in the country at the time. Disraeli informed the Queen that he expected Britain would be restored to 'her due and natural influence in the government of the world.'[33] However, matters became complicated during the course of the summer of 1876 as news reached Britain of the ferocious methods used by the Turks to suppress an uprising in Bulgaria, which left perhaps 15,000 dead. Disraeli was initially sceptical about the accuracy of the reports being published in the newspapers, and he made a number of dismissive remarks about them in public, including his notorious reference to 'coffee-house babble'. Such comments were soon to appear flippant and callous, and they rebounded badly on Disraeli when it became clear that atrocities really had been committed against the Bulgarians. More seriously still, the Bulgarian atrocities provided the focus for a protest movement in the country in which Radicals, working men's organisations and nonconformists played a prominent part. By September, the fomer Liberal leader, Gladstone, had emerged from his retirement to condemn the immorality of Disraeli's conduct in failing to co-operate with the European Powers in order to coerce the Turks into making concessions. The bitter rivalry between Disraeli and Gladstone was thus renewed.

It is probably the case that Gladstone's involvement in the Bulgarian agitation tended to harden Disraeli's attitude on the opposite side, so that the latter became increasingly pro-Turkish in his views. In effect, Disraeli resurrected the old 'Palmerstonian' policy of the Crimean War period (1854–6), which held that it was in Britain's interests to help preserve the Turkish Empire as a bulwark against Russian expans-ionism. The reasoning behind Disraeli's stance was that Russia might exploit the opportunity provided by the Balkan uprisings to justify her intervention in the region, posing as the champion of the oppressed Slav peoples. In this way, it was feared, Russia would move a step closer to its goal of capturing Constantinople (Istanbul) itself, and once a presence had been established in the eastern Mediterranean it would be possible for Russia to threaten Britain's sea route to India via the Suez Canal. Whether Disraeli's assessment of Britain's interests in relation to the Eastern Question was rational, is certainly open to doubt: it could be argued that a better approach would have been to support the creation of a group of independent Balkan states as a more effective barrier against Russia than the Turks could provide. It may also be true that the British obsession with the threat to her route to India was exaggerated.[34] Nevertheless, the practical result of Disraeli's policy was to encourage the Turks to resist the diplomatic pressure for concessions that was brought to bear on her at a conference of the European Powers held at Constantinople at the end of 1876.

Disraeli's identification with an independent, belligerent and self-interested British foreign policy may only have occurred in the last years of his career,[35] but the fact that he should have made a pitch for 'patriotic' feeling in the country was entirely in keeping with his character. As Lord Derby, the Foreign Secretary, who personally favoured a non-interventionist policy, observed in his journal in October 1876, 'To the Premier the main thing is to please and surprise the public by bold strokes and unexpected moves: he would rather run serious national risks than hear his policy called feeble or commonplace.'[36] Similarly, at the end of 1877, Derby complained to a colleague that their chief 'believes thoroughly in "prestige" as all foreigners do, and would think it (quite sincerely) in the interests of the country to spend 200 millions on a war if the result was to make foreign States think more highly of us as a military power.'[37] Eventually, Disraeli's theatrical urge to make an impact on European diplomacy and thereby win applause at home, even at the risk of engaging in a war with Russia, proved too much for Derby and Carnarvon, who both resigned from the government in the early months of 1878.

Despite the moralistic public outcry against the Bulgarian atrocities in the autumn of 1876, subsequent events suggested that there was indeed a plentiful supply of 'patriotic' sentiment in the country susceptible to the appeal of Disraeli's brand of *realpolitik*. When Russia unilaterally declared war on Turkey in April 1877, the reaction in Britain was a violent wave of anti-Russian feeling, manifested most notoriously in the popular music hall song by 'The Great MacDermott' (George Farrell), which introduced the word 'Jingo' into the English language.[38]

> The Dogs of War are loose and the rugged Russian Bear,
>
> Full bent on blood and robbery has crawled out of his lair...
>
> As peacemaker old England her very utmost tried,
>
> The Russians said they wanted peace, but then those Russians lied,
>
> Of carnage and of trickery they'll have sufficient feast,
>
> Ere they dare to think of coming near our Road into the East.
>
> *Chorus*
>
> We don't want to fight, but by Jingo if we do
>
> We've got the ships, we've got the men, and got the money too.
>
> We've fought the Bear before, and while we're Britons true,
>
> The Russians shall not have Constantinople.

Britain did not actually fight, but preserved her neutrality until it became clear what the outcome of the war was going to be. The crisis point was reached early in 1878, when Turkish military resistance finally collapsed and the British government sought an emergency vote of credit (£6 million) from Parliament to make preparations in case Russia occupied Constantinople.

In the event, Russia held back from the Turkish capital, but it was during this tense period in late January and early February, when war seemed imminent, that public demonstrations in favour of an uncompromising British stance were at their height. Meetings organised by peace campaigners were broken up, and Gladstone, the most prominent critic of Disraeli's policy, became a popular hate figure: the windows of his London home were smashed, and he was burned in effigy at various gatherings. Pro-government demonstrations were heavily concentrated in certain areas, notably London, the West Midlands and Northwest England, and they were very much an urban, not a rural, phenomenon. 'Jingoism' was evidently attractive to various groups of people, such as those working in the financial sector in the City of London (especially the Stock Exchange), half-pay army officers, 'swells' (expensively dressed men from the 'leisured' classes), government clerks, dockers (some of them unemployed), workers from the munitions industry, medical students (a notoriously rowdy element) and other youths looking for some excitement. There was indeed a carnival atmosphere at many meetings, helped along by bonfires, brass bands and beer. However, as the authority on jingoism has concluded, it was 'an ephemeral force...based on disparate groups whose patriotism derived from different sources,' and by the spring of 1878 the jingo passion seems to have largely subsided.[39]

Diplomatic events, meanwhile, were moving in Disraeli's favour. Russia had unwisely imposed a drastic peace settlement on Turkey (the treaty of San Stefano), which, if implemented, would have ended the Turkish presence in Europe and set up a large client Bulgarian state. Britain responded with a series of military gestures designed to threaten the Russians: the fleet was ordered to Constantinople, the army reserves were called out at home, and 7,000 Indian troops were stationed on Malta. Fortunately, perhaps, for Disraeli's government, its military resolve was never tested. The treaty of San Stefano was equally unacceptable to Austria, and with two of the members of the Dreikaiserbund thus at loggerheads, Germany was anxious to broker an agreement. Russia, under formidable diplomatic and military pressure, was obliged to submit the treaty for revision by a Congress of the European Powers held at Berlin in June–July 1878.

The Congress of Berlin was unquestionably Disraeli's finest hour, affording him a magnificent opportunity to occupy centre-stage in the councils of Europe and thus ending (albeit temporarily) Britain's international isolation. Furthermore, the terms of the revised peace settlement were agreeable to Disraeli. A smaller, independent Bulgaria was created, but Turkey retained a presence in Europe, while Britain, as the result of a separate convention with the Turks, guaranteed their possessions in Asia in return for the acquisition of Cyprus. Disraeli was therefore able to return to London in triumph as an international statesman, claiming 'peace with honour'.

Politically speaking, the Eastern Question had been of great advantage to Disraeli for the way it divided his opponents while rallying the Conservative Party to his support. Gladstone, it is true, had re-emerged as a dangerous critic of the government, but he was not the official leader of the Liberals, and nor were his idealistic, 'peacemongering' views representative of the whole of his party. In fact, many Liberals, including the House of Commons leader, Hartington, substantially approved of Disraeli's course and were throughout the crisis reluctant to engage in outright opposition to him. As a result, the Liberals were thrown into a state of chaos in Parliament. On the other hand, the protracted political emergency arising from the Eastern Question, together with the resentment felt at the attacks made on Disraeli by Gladstone and other 'unpatriotic' Liberals, had had a wholly beneficial influence on the cohesion of the Conservatives. The diary of Speaker Brand confirms that 'the supporters of Ministers have always shewn a united front.'[40] In the summer of 1878, therefore, Disraeli's personal position appeared to be stronger than ever before.

Towards defeat, 1878–80

The natural question for Disraeli's government, after the successful resolution of the crisis in the East, was whether or not to capitalise on its apparent public approval by requesting an early dissolution of Parliament. While the political advantages of a general election were obvious, there were also serious objections to the adoption of such a course. Parliamentary elections were still governed by the Septennial Act of 1716, which required a dissolution every seven years, but the current Parliament was only four-and-a-half years old and it was the established convention to allow them to run at least into their sixth year. An early general election could have been justified if the government was unable to command a working majority in the House of Commons, but this was clearly not a problem for Disraeli's ministry. Furthermore, as the Chief Whip, Sir William Hart Dyke, pointed out, requiring Conservative MPs to face the expense of elections prematurely would have been a poor way of rewarding their loyalty in the division lobbies. Other important considerations, though, were the worrying state of the economy, which had experienced an acute depression since 1876, and the government's urgent need to reduce its expenditure in order to ease the burden of taxation (the income tax had been raised to 5d. in the pound in 1878). At a Cabinet meeting on 10 August, Lord Sandon records that Disraeli and Northcote spoke strongly in favour of government retrenchment, now that the threat of war had been lifted, and 'Cross spoke strongly also in this direction... adding, which I confirmed, that he believed this question of economy was one of life and death to the Party and Government.' This view was subsequently echoed by the Chief Whip, who advised Disraeli to delay the general election until the Country had recovered from the slump and the government was able to restore its finances on to a sound footing.[41]

With the benefit of hindsight, it is easy to say that Disraeli and his colleagues made a serious miscalculation in not going to the Country immediately, but they could not have anticipated that the economic depression would intensify during the latter part of 1878 and through 1879. Many businesses went bankrupt, industrial unemployment continued to rise, and attempts by employers to impose wage reductions provoked an increasing number of strikes. Agricultural prosperity, meanwhile, was being shattered by the effects of cheap imports from the USA which compounded the problems caused by a succession of bad harvests.

Disraeli's ministry, it became quite clear, had no response to this worsening situation. It is a good indication of how limited the scope for positive action by late-Victorian governments was perceived to be, that the only constructive suggestion considered by the Cabinet at the end of 1878 was that they should initiate a voluntary national subscription to help provide relief for the distressed population, somewhat along the lines of the fund raised during the Lancashire cotton famine of the early 1860s. Disraeli was interested in the idea but he gave way to the arguments of his Chancellor of the Exchequer, who feared that the proposed subscription might set a bad precedent for the future, raising working-class expectations of a permanent system of charitable assistance. There was nothing else for it, Northcote argued, but to wait for better times to return.[42] Disraeli proved no more able to challenge the prevailing commercial orthodoxy of the time, which dictated that Britain should adhere to its free trade system regardless of the effects of cheap foreign competition on agriculture and other industries like iron and steel. Remembering Disraeli's condemnation of Peel in the 1840s, it is painfully ironic that he himself should have been Prime Minister when the long-term consequences of Free Trade for British agriculturalists finally made themselves felt, and yet was unable to devise any solution to the plight of his staunchest supporters. There were calls for a restoration of tariffs, so that farmers could obtain a better price for their crops, but Disraeli could scarcely contemplate a policy designed to protect the interests of producers, at the expense of consumers, when the Conservatives' own Reform Act of 1867 had enfranchised large numbers of urban working-class consumers wanting cheap food.

The Conservatives thus found themselves governing in an increasingly hostile economic and political environment. Beyond this, there was the simple fact that Disraeli was exhausted: attendance at the Berlin Congress had imposed a great strain on his already fragile health, and he had very nearly broken down; thereafter, he was frequently unwell. Disraeli's decrepitude seemed to transmit itself to the rest of his government, particularly in the House of Commons, where Northcote's good-natured but infirm leadership was unequal to the task of coping with the obstructionist tactics employed by Irish Home Rulers like Charles Stewart Parnell (often aided by radical Liberals). The 1879 session therefore turned out to be legislatively barren. Northcote's budget did not help the government's position, as he was forced to resort to borrowing through the issue of exchequer bonds in order to cover his deficit without raising the income tax still further. (In 1880 he raided the Sinking Fund, intended for reducing the national debt, to achieve the same result.) Such steps inevitably outraged the Liberals' sense of financial propriety. The Opposition was also much more united by 1879, thanks to the unfortunate military escapades against the Afghans and Zulus, which provided an easy target for Liberal criticism and further discredited the government.

In the Scottish county constituency of Midlothian, at the end of 1879, Disraeli's greatest political enemy, Gladstone, delivered a blistering critique of the government's policies in a famous series of speeches. Gladstone's message to his newly-adopted constituency, where he had agreed to challenge the incumbent Conservative MP at the general election, was that the numerous sins of ministers were not simply a collection of individual misdemeanours but an inevitable consequence of a pernicious *system* of misrule to which he applied the label 'Beaconsfieldism' (Disraeli, it will be recalled, was now the Earl of Beaconsfield). According to Gladstone, the government was responsible for military atrocities committed against innocent tribespeople in Afghanistan and Southern Africa, which were both immoral and quite unnecessary, being the result of a restless urge to interfere in the affairs of other nations. Having condemned Disraeli's brand of imperialism, Gladstone proceeded to show how the heavy military expenditure it involved had produced a mounting budget deficit, which Northcote was trying to tackle with dubious financial expedients. Moreover, the government's extravagant wastefulness had made it necessary to increase taxes, placing a crippling burden on the economy and contributing, along with the government's meddlesome and disruptive overseas policy itself, to the bad state of trade. Disraeli was thus found guilty of inspiring a wicked and senseless policy of imperial aggrandisement and glorification, for which the country was now paying a heavy price.

It may seem surprising that, after the Gladstonian onslaught at Midlothian, Disraeli and his colleagues failed to make any public response, and yet, only three months later, in March 1880, chose to request a dissolution of Parliament, when they could have waited until the autumn. The explanation for the Conservative leadership's disinclination to challenge Gladstone on the public platform lies partly in a personal distaste for 'stumping' the country (Disraeli himself, in any case, was not physically up to the task) and partly in the belief that Gladstone had mistimed his campaign and risked peaking too soon. In fact, it was the government's intention at the beginning of 1880 to delay the general election until later in the year, but two misleading by-election victories at Liverpool and Southwark in February inspired false Conservative confidence that Gladstone's Midlothian demonstration was already a spent force. The party managers predicted that an immediate dissolution would result in only a modest loss of seats, leaving the Conservatives with a small overall majority in the next Parliament.[43] On 8 March, therefore, Disraeli sprang a sudden general election on the Country, which was almost as unexpected as Gladstone's announcement in January 1874.

Disraeli's election address took the form of a public letter to the Lord Lieutenant of Ireland, the Duke of Marlborough, in which he warned that the existence of the United Kingdom was being jeopardised by the disreputable conduct of the Liberals, who had (allegedly) aligned themselves with the

Parnellite Home Rulers. In Disraeli's view, Liberal coquetting with Irish nationalism was part of a wider, sinister design to 'enfeeble our colonies by [a] policy of decomposition.' The British Empire, in other words, would be endangered by the return of a Liberal government.[44] Disraeli may well have been prompted to adopt this line of attack by events in the recent Liverpool by-election, where the Liberal candidate's attempt to capture the considerable Irish vote, by stating that he would support an inquiry into the demand for Home Rule, had produced a Protestant–Unionist backlash in this volatile city, to the benefit of the Conservatives. In national terms, however, Disraeli's address did not have the desired effect of alarming the electorate, and it appeared instead as if he was merely creating a smokescreen with which to obscure other issues more damaging to his government.

By 4 April, one of Disraeli's Cabinet colleagues was writing in his diary that 'The defeat...is most disastrous & complete... the thunder has come from a clear sky!'[45] The scale of the Conservatives' losses was found to be even more disastrous once the results from the county constituencies were all declared. One historian has estimated that the Liberals won 353 seats to the Conservatives' 238, while the Home Rulers emerged 61 strong.[46] The government fared particularly badly in the 'Celtic fringe', suffering a net loss of 36 seats, so that they were reduced to only two MPs in Wales, seven in Scotland, and 23 in Ireland (all but five of these representing Ulster seats). Heavy casualties were sustained in the English boroughs, with the gains made in the largest constituencies at the previous election, being completely wiped out. More alarming still was the net loss of 27 English county seats, which was partially attributable to the agitation by the Farmers' Alliance, a pressure group campaigning for reforms in the system of land tenure. With the Liberals exploiting the inevitable friction in the relations between landlords and farmers at a time of acute agricultural depression, it appeared as if the mainstay of Conservative support in their traditional county strongholds was being eroded. Lancashire, where the Conservatives had done so well in 1868 and 1874, also turned against the government, and eight borough and four county seats were lost. Only in London and the Home Counties did the Conservatives manage to hold on to some of the ground gained in recent years.

Disraeli's assessment of the electoral disaster in April 1880 was that it was mainly due to 'Hard Times',[47] a consoling thought for any defeated politician, but probably an accurate estimate of the situation in this case. Much blame was also put on the supposedly run-down state of Conservative organisation in the constituencies, but even if this view was justified the problem was presumably only a symptom of the general malaise afflicting a demoralised governing party in severe difficulties. The uncomfortable thought remained that perhaps the great Conservative victory of 1874 had been an exceptional result, facilitated by an unusually favourable combination of circumstances, and that the party would have to readjust its political horizons and concentrate on that dreary task of long-term opposition to Liberal governments which it had performed for so much of the mid-Victorian era. Gladstone, who had triumphed in the Midlothian contest, overrode the claims of Hartington to the Premiership and received the commission to form the new government from a distraught Queen Victoria. For Disraeli, there was the painful awareness that his detested rival had triumphed over him, in the final act, and that he was unlikely to see his vision of a 'national' Conservative party fully realised in his lifetime.

5

DISRAELI'S ACHIEVEMENT

The final year

Disraeli died almost exactly a year after leaving office. He remained the leader of his party until the end, having pledged his continued service to the Conservative cause at a gathering of some 500 peers and MPs held at Bridgewater House on 19 May 1880. Disraeli warned the meeting that Gladstone's ministry posed a serious threat to the power of the aristocracy, because of its dependence on the support of 'revolutionaries' (i.e. Radicals), on the backbenches, whose first target was sure to be the system of land tenure. He therefore advised the Conservative Party to support the government whenever possible, in order to encourage it to resist such dangerous pressures. Trying to take an optimistic view of the future, he reminded his audience of how quickly Earl Grey's Whig administration had lost its popularity after carrying the Great Reform Act, implying that a similar process of disintegration was likely to afflict the Gladstonian Liberals.[1] Shortly after the meeting, in a letter to Lord Lytton, Disraeli maintained that it was his wish to retire from public life, but only when a suitable successor had emerged. In the meantime, he was resolved to 'act as if I were still young & vigorous, & take all steps in my power to sustain the spirit & restore the discipline of the Tory party. They have existed for more than a century & a half as an organised political connection &...they must not be snuffed out.'[2]

From his position in the House of Lords, Disraeli generally adopted a cautious approach to the new government's legislation, recognising as he did the dangers of being seen to obstruct ministers with the force of a fresh electoral mandate behind them. He therefore counselled the Conservative peers not to reject the Ground Game Bill, giving tenant farmers full power to destroy hares and rabbits on their holdings, even though privately he detested this measure, which interfered in the contractual relations between landlords and tenants in a spirit, apparently, of wishing to inflame such relations. An Employers' Liability Bill providing greater protection for workmen involved in industrial accidents was also allowed to pass. However, Disraeli and the Conservatives took a very belligerent line against the government's Irish Compensation for Disturbance Bill, which penalised Irish landlords who evicted their tenants. This Bill was produced in an attempt to stabilise Ireland's agrarian society, which was suffering particularly badly from the effects of the depression in agriculture, but to the outraged Conservatives it seemed that Gladstone and his colleagues were out to victimise the landlord class and that the measure would also set a perilous precedent for English landowners. With the assistance of a large number of equally alarmed Whig peers, the Conservatives were able to inflict a heavy defeat on the government's bill on 3 August. But as conditions in Ireland continued to deteriorate, during the autumn of 1880, it became clear that further land legislation could be expected in the next parliamentary session. 'With nearly 50 years experience of public affairs', Disraeli wrote to Lord Cairns at the end of October, 'I confess I look on the present with anxiety — not to say gloom', and he became increasingly despondent about the possibility of successfully resisting another Gladstonian assault on the Irish landlords.[3]

Disraeli's fears for the future security of the traditional ruling class are reflected in the fragment of a new novel, presumably to have been called *Falconet*, which was left among his papers at the time of his death.[4] The character of Falconet was obviously based on none other than Gladstone himself, being depicted as arrogant, priggish, humourless, rigid in his religious creed, with a 'disputatious temper', and in command of an unstoppable flow of oratory. It is unclear how the plot was meant to develop, but the introduction of a number of characters espousing revolutionary, nihilistic beliefs suggests that Disraeli's mind was much preoccupied with the supposedly destructive tendencies of Gladstonian rule.

Appropriately enough, Disraeli's last appearance in the House of Lords, on 15 March 1881, was in order to support a vote of condolence following the assassination by Russian nihilists of Tsar Alexander II. Equally appropriate, perhaps, was the fact that the atrocious winter of 1880–1, which inflicted yet further damage on British agriculture, upon whose prosperity the territorial ruling class depended so much, also killed Disraeli. A chill caught one night when he was returning from dinner developed into bronchitis, and he died on 19 April at his recently-acquired London house in Curzon Street. The terms of his will precluded the public burial which Gladstone had felt obliged to offer, and Disraeli was interred, according to his instructions, next to his wife at Hughenden Church.

The late-Victorian Conservative Party

At the time of his death, Disraeli's legacy to the Conservative party appeared to be ambiguous. It was true that in 1874 he had helped to secure the party's first overall parliamentary majority for a generation, and that six eventful years in government had followed, but the 1880 general election was a catastrophe for the Conservatives, who found themselves back at square one as the party of Opposition. More worrying still was the suggestion that the party faced major structural problems, arising from the erosion of the economic power of the territorial ruling class, which threatened to undermine the Conservatives' electoral influence in many rural constituencies.

The Gladstone ministry's appetite for intrusive land legislation in Ireland seemed to point the way to the eventual fate of English landowners, and it was also expected that the Liberals would seek to make further inroads into the Conservatives' county strongholds by enfranchising the agricultural labourers (indeed, such a measure was passed in 1884). Thus, in April 1881, there was an ominous possibility that the political authority of the landed elite, which Disraeli had dedicated his career to upholding, was about to collapse, and that the Conservative party, which Disraeli had sought to establish as the 'national' party, might never be in a position to form a strong government again.

In retrospect, of course, we can see that the outlook for the Conservatives was much more promising than contemporaries thought in 1881. At the next general election, in 1885, the party achieved a remarkable transformation in its position by winning a majority of seats in the English *boroughs* and they consolidated their hold over these constituencies at subsequent elections up to 1900. Admittedly, the Liberal menace in the counties seemed to be growing in 1885, but the Conservatives recovered a good deal of ground the following year, and they were reasonably effective in containing the Liberals for some time thereafter. It was primarily due to the Conservatives' new-found borough strength that they were able to inflict heavy electoral defeats on their opponents in 1886, 1895 and 1900. The key to the Conservatives' success in the boroughs lies in the details of the Franchise and Redistribution reforms of 1884–5, which included a substantial transfer of seats from small boroughs (where the Liberals had always done well) to London and other major urban centres, giving them a representation more in proportion to the size of their populations. Single-member constituencies were also introduced in most places. These provisions worked to the Conservatives' advantage, enabling them to maximise the electoral potential of their growing middle-class support, especially in London (even the 1880 election had only partially checked this), while the creation of single-member seats assisted this process by providing the Conservatives with a number of predominantly middle-class constituencies in the business and suburban districts of all the big cities, where they could hope to do well. The credit for securing these changes was largely due to the man rapidly emerging as Disraeli's likely successor in the Conservative leadership, Lord Salisbury, who had made effective use of the political leverage supplied by the Conservatives' majority in the House of Lords, blocking any reform of the county franchise until Gladstone agreed to negotiate with him the terms of the accompanying redistribution of seats. Salisbury thus secured a favourable redistribution settlement which, as it turned out, more than offset the disadvantages of household suffrage in the counties.[5]

However, it is far from certain that the Conservatives' political ascendancy in the late Victorian period could have been achieved without the Liberal schism of 1886, provoked by Gladstone's attempt to grant Home Rule to Ireland. Disraeli may be said to have been prescient in this respect, for he had tried to focus public attention on the threat to the United Kingdom from the Home Rule movement at the time of the 1880 General Election. His warning was not heeded then, but the policy of resistance to Irish nationalism proved to be a potent political issue for the Conservatives within a few years of his death. Gladstone's Home Rule Bill, introduced in 1886, probably served to accelerate the middle-class drift towards Conservatism in the constituencies, while the party was reinforced in Parliament by the defection of nearly 100 'Liberal Unionist' MPs — a mixture of aristocratic Whigs, businessmen and middle-class professionals. The resulting alliance between Conservatives and Liberal Unionists dominated British politics for the next twenty years. Its anti-Home Rule stance was linked to wider concerns about the maintenance of the empire, at a time when Britain and other European States were engaged in a scramble for colonial territory in Africa and the Pacific. The ideological basis of late-Victorian Conservatism can therefore reasonably be described as 'Disraelian' in inspiration.

During the last two decades of the nineteenth century the Conservatives continued to evolve into a party embracing the interests of all owners of property, urban as well as rural. Most historians have taken the view that Disraeli's contribution to this process was made by adopting an essentially 'Peelite' policy, based on an adherence to orthodox Free Trade maxims, combined with a cautious approach to State intervention in the field of social reform. In this way, the propertied classes were to be reassured that the Conservatives were a 'responsible' party of government. Disraeli, it is therefore argued, presided over the creation of a modern 'Conservative' party, despite the fact that he had worked to prevent Peel from achieving the same objective in the 1840s.[6] This interpretation certainly has some validity to it, provided we recognise that the middle classes were a far larger and more diverse force by the 1870s and 1880s than they had been in Peel's day, and that the threat from radicalism was taking a more 'socialistic' form in the late 19th century than it had in the 1840s. Disraeli, it may be felt, succeeded where Peel had failed because the social and political environment in which he was operating was more conducive to the fulfilment of a 'Conservative' strategy.

On the other hand, a case can be made for the view that there was also an important 'Tory' component to late-Victorian Conservatism. If the Conservative Party was to flourish in an increasingly democratic system — after the 1884 Reform Act, about 60 per cent of adult males were able to vote — it was not enough simply to be the party of property: the Conservatives needed to cultivate a genuinely populist appeal as well. Disraeli had always asserted that the Conservatives were the party of the whole nation, and after his death the anti-Home Rule and pro-imperial cries helped to give fresh substance to this political self-image. Curiously enough, Disraeli was to have a significant posthumous role to play in this respect, through the activities of the Primrose League, founded in his memory in 1883. (The primrose was supposed to be his favourite flower.) The League became a mass political organisation, with a membership of one million, by 1891, and it proved a valuable electoral asset for the Conservative Party, supplying large numbers of voluntary campaign workers. Individual Primrose League 'habitations' were structured along medieval, hierarchical lines, with ranks such as 'knights', 'esquires' and 'dames'. Much of the emphasis was placed on organising social functions like dances and fêtes, but the purpose was to inculcate feelings of loyalty and reverence towards the Crown, the Empire, and other institutions.[7] No doubt, the social deference thus instilled into the minds of large numbers of ordinary people would have appealed to Disraeli's Young England instincts. An updated version of 'Tory Democracy', it seems, was being formulated to suit the political conditions of the 1880s and 1890s, and the mystique surrounding Conservative memories of what Disraeli had (supposedly) stood for equipped the party with a useful weapon with which to combat Gladstone's demagogic Liberalism.

The question of consistency

Leaving aside Disraeli's contribution to the success of late-Victorian Conservatism, whatever one may consider that to have been, he usually stands charged by historians with political opportunism, on the grounds that he lacked any clear, guiding principles and was willing to change his policies and vary his alliances in the pursuit of power. It is difficult to dispute the view that Disraeli was an adventurer, when we recall his dubious transition from radicalism to Toryism in the 1830s; or the way that he lauded Peel at the start of his parliamentary career but turned against him in the 1840s when he was not given office; how he opposed the repeal of the Corn Laws and yet quickly abandoned the protectionist cause; and how he then devoted much of his energy in the 1850s to the search for political alignments with groups as diverse as the Peelites, the Whigs, the Radicals and the Irish Brigade. One can only add, by way of mitigation, that the mature political leader of the 1860s and 1870s was usually much more circumspect, and willing to be patient, rather than desperately grabbing at political power whenever it came near.

The Disraeli of 1873, who declined to form a government because he believed the time was not yet ripe, was clearly a far wiser creature than its forebear of twenty years earlier.

There are two respects, however, in which it is possible to argue that Disraeli displayed great consistency throughout his career. Firstly, there is little reason to doubt that Disraeli was consistent in his overall political objective — that is to say, his sense of the purpose of devoting his life to politics did not change. He sought personal glory, of course, but in doing so he dedicated himself to the preservation of the territorial aristocracy, whose traditional political leadership Disraeli believed was both a guarantee of the rights and liberties of the people, great and small, and the foundation of Britain's greatness among the nations of the world. It was shown in Chapter 1 how Disraeli succeeded in identifying himself, emotionally, with the aristocracy because of, rather than in spite of, his peculiar notions about his Jewish heritage. In a famous letter to Lord Stanley (later the 14th Earl of Derby), written at the beginning of their long political association, in 1848, Disraeli stated that:

> The office of leader of the Conservative party in the H of C at the present day is to uphold the aristocratic settlement of this country. That is the only question at stake, however manifold may be the forms which it assumes in public discussion, and however various the knowledge & the labor which it requires.[8]

It might reasonably be objected that Disraeli was allowing himself considerable scope for discretion here, in that any short-term tactic or manoeuvre could have been justified by reference to the long-term strategy which he had defined, and it is certainly true that Derby had to stifle some of the more 'flexible' projects put forward by his over-zealous lieutenant (see Chapter 2). All the same, Disraeli's sincere commitment to the cause of aristocratic government does help to explain how and why he gradually shifted his political ground, after becoming Conservative leader in the Commons, by accepting both the Whig constitutional settlement of the 1830s and the Peelite/Liberal Free Trade commercial settlement of the

1840s, in the hope of harnessing the middle classes to the support of the nation's institutions. Disraeli, it can therefore be said, pursued the same goals even when he was adapting himself to fit in with changing political conditions.[9]

Secondly, there is a remarkable continuity in the rhetoric which Disraeli employed, from the time of his first attempts to gain entry to the House of Commons in the 1830s right up until his death. Disraeli's essential message, invariably, was that the party to which he adhered was the 'national' party and that its mission was to thwart the sinister and pernicious designs of the opposing party. This 'national' party invariably stood for the maintenance of traditional institutions like the Crown, the Church and the House of Lords, and it was resolved to uphold the empire of England, but it also wished to ameliorate (in ways usually unspecified) the condition of the people.[10] We saw in Chapter 1 how Disraeli developed a personal interpretation of English history which enabled him to identify the menace posed to the nation's greatness and thus justify his own political course. In the 1830s, the 'oligarchical' Whigs, with their 'anti-national' policies designed to emasculate the Crown and other institutions, and with their callous approach to social issues like the Poor Law, were clearly the culprits; by the mid-1840s, Peel and his perverted brand of 'Conservatism' (merely Liberalism in disguise), was judged to be equally dangerous; while in 1872, the problem lay with the 'cosmopolitan' principles of Gladstone's Ministry, representing the climax of a forty-year period of Liberal rule in which the nation's institutions had been systematically assailed. Nothing had really changed in 1880, when Disraeli alleged that the Liberals had entered into a sordid compact with the Irish Home Rulers, thereby jeopardising the security of the United Kingdom and of the empire itself.

Disraelian myths

It has already been suggested that Disraeli's legacy must be judged, to some extent, in posthumous terms, as it is not

141

merely what he actually did that counts but what subsequent generations of Conservatives made of him. The memory of Disraeli has indeed been a fertile source of inspiration for his political descendants, and the process of mythologisation was already under way in the 1880s. For instance, the journalist, T. E. Kebbel, in his *History of Toryism* (1886), declared that Disraeli's career had been based on a consistent application of the principles enunciated in his Young England novels, and that he had 'made it the business of his life to close up the gap in our social system which...[had] gradually been widening, and to reconcile the working classes to the Throne, the Church and the Aristocracy.' According to Kebbel, 'The Reform Bill of 1867...was the making of the Tory Party', as it 'gave them a position which they required for dealing with the social problems of the age.' In his great ministry of 1874–80, Disraeli had therefore had the rare pleasure of being able to redress those 'social wrongs' which he had described in his youth.[11] Conservative politicians were also making good use of Disraeli, notably Lord Randolph Churchill and his associates in the so-called 'Fourth Party', a backbench ginger group, who identified themselves with the notion of 'Tory Democracy'. This term had not been used in Disraeli's own time, but it was supposed to represent a continuation of his political principles, above all his faith in the loyalty of the masses.[12] Incidentally, Churchill and his friends were responsible for founding the Primrose League, although this organisation was quickly taken under the wing of the official party managers. A good indication of how quickly the mythology of 'Tory Democracy' took root in the minds of Conservatives is provided by the fact that in the 1890s the renegade Radical, Joseph Chamberlain, who had allied himself with the Conservatives via the Liberal Unionist party, attempted to propagate a programme of welfare measures, including old age pensions, by claiming that he was acting in the spirit of the Disraelian tradition of social reform.[13]

With the publication between 1910 and 1920 of W. F. Monypenny and G. E. Buckle's six volume official biography of Disraeli, using his private papers, a monument was erected to the deceased Conservative leader which added substantial intellectual respectability to the study of his life. Disraeli was presented as the man who had reminded his party that 'it had its origins in high and national ideas', and who ably carried forward those ideas by helping to consolidate the empire and improve the condition of the people. In Monypenny and Buckle's estimate, Disraeli's career had demonstrated 'exceptional greatness, only just short of supreme mastery'. He had been 'a grand and magnificent figure, standing solitary, towering above his contemporaries…[a] man of fervid imagination and vision wide and deep, amid a nation of narrow practical minds'.[14]

For several decades to come, this heroic version of Disraeli's achievement had a profound influence on other Conservative writers. It became a commonplace view that Disraeli had revived the authentic traditions of his party: thus he 'guide[d] the Conservative Party back to its true course'; or he recalled Conservatism to the 'great heritage of Toryism'.[15] This authentic tradition was encapsulated in the slogan 'one nation'. Thanks to Disraeli, the working classes had been inspired with a love for the country's great institutions and, as the political embodiment of these popular loyalties, the Conservatives had become, just as Disraeli had always said they must, the 'national party', a truly classless entity. As one writer in the 1930s put it, 'Disraeli had a profound trust in the British working man. He was the great 'tory democrat' of his day.'[16] Disraeli had recognised that 'the working-class stream is but a large tributary of the main national river',[17] and he was even credited with a 'penetrating vision…[a] power of interpreting the general will', which enabled 'the great statesman [to become] a seer and draw men to him.'[18]

Central to the Conservatives' 'one nation' image, of course, was the legacy of concern for social reform inherited from Disraeli. In his Young England days, Disraeli had drawn attention to the 'intolerable social evils' arising from the Industrial Revolution, and he had repudiated the doctrines of laissez-faire, based on irresponsible individualism, teaching instead that England was an 'organic' society in which men of all classes had duties towards one another.[19] Many Conservative writers of the inter-war period clearly found it helpful to appeal to the Disraelian social reform tradition, at a time when the menace of socialism was becoming very real in the form of a Labour party which had superseded the Liberals as the party of the 'left' in British politics. The claims made by Arthur Bryant in 1929 seem preposterous now, but they may have been effective enough at the time at which he wrote:

> When Disraeli recreated the Conservative Party, it was on a national policy that should secure to the peasant a holding and a stake in the land, to the industrial classes in the great towns decent conditions of health, housing and civic life, and to every citizen a system of local self-government...The newly-formed Socialist Party has taken to itself much of the 'social reform' programme of Disraelian Conservatism, but has never perhaps clearly understood its object.[20]

In the aftermath of the Second World War Disraeli continued to prove his utility to the Conservative cause as a source of legitimacy for those, such as Harold Macmillan and R. A. Butler, who were anxious to adapt their party's policies to suit the new environment created by the Attlee government's programme of economic management and welfarism. For Macmillan, indeed, Disraeli was a political hero, and he frequently appealed to the Disraelian tradition of Conservatism in his speeches.[21] It may not be entirely absurd, therefore, to describe Disraeli as an indirect architect of the post-war 'consensus' in British politics which lasted until the 1970s.

Sadly for Disraeli, his reputation has been seriously diminished in the past thirty years or so. A generation of professional historians, writing in the 1960s, set about puncturing the mythology surrounding Disraeli's name: readers now learned, for example, that he was essentially an opportunist and an impresario, that the second Reform Act was not founded on any vision of a 'Tory Democracy', that his leadership of the Conservative party had actually been insecure right up until the 1874 election victory, that he was not the prophet of the 'new imperialism', and that he showed very little interest in the practical details of social reform — which were, in any case, emphatically not derived from the principles espoused in his Young England novels.[22] In the meantime, the researches of Professor Gash had prompted an upwardly-revised estimate of the political stature of Sir Robert Peel, the man whose leadership Disraeli had played such a crucial part in destroying. Peel now emerged as a politician of high principles, an economic moderniser, a great consensual leader and, in spite of what happened in 1846, the real founder of 'modern Conservatism'.[23] More recently, historians have even found a good word to say about the 14th Earl of Derby, who for decades had almost entirely dropped out of view, but whose long custodianship of the mid-Victorian Conservative Party is now seen as laying the foundations for Disraeli's later success.[24] The impact of much of this historical revisionism coincided with a shift towards the 'right' in Conservative politics, associated with the rise of Margaret Thatcher, whose reaction against the 'one nation' policies of her predecessors, Macmillan and Heath, and preference for 'conviction' politics, ensured that there was no hallowed place for Disraeli in the new Conservative pantheon. It was left to 'wets' like Sir Ian Gilmour, critical of 'Thatcherism', to keep the flame of Disraeli's memory flickering.[25]

It is naturally tempting to speculate as to the likelihood of the Conservatives' rediscovering their Disraelian heritage as part of the process of redefining the nature of their party for the 21st century. From a historian's point of view, however, there are definite advantages in being able to approach a complex subject like the life of Disraeli free from the intellectual constraints imposed by the weight of political folk-memory or current partisan loyalties. It is to be hoped that this short book will encourage students simply to appreciate Disraeli for what he was, a self-made exponent of the virtues of aristocratic government, a supremely talented parliamentarian and a political leader gifted with powers of imagination.

REFERENCES

1 IMAGINATION AND POLITICS

1 Disraeli's election address, 1 July 1837, in J. Matthews and M. G. Wiebe (eds.), *Benjamin Disraeli Letters* (University of Toronto Press, 1982), Vol. II, No. 629.

2 For the whole of this section, see Robert Blake, *Disraeli* (London, 1966), chs. 1–6.

3 It is true, of course, that Jews could not sit in parliament until 1858, but there were several instances before Disraeli of Jewish converts to Anglicanism becoming MPs. It has recently been argued that, while Disraeli as a politician was always a target for anti-semitic abuse, this became much more virulent during his Premiership in the 1870s. Anthony S. Wohl, '"Dizzi-Ben-Dizzi": Disraeli as Alien', *Journal of British Studies*, XXXIV (1995), pp. 375–411.

4 Stanley Weintraub, *Disraeli: A Biography* (London, 1993), p. 38.

5 Blake, *Disraeli*, p. 59.

6 *Disraeli Letters,* Vol. I, Appendix 3.

7 Disraeli to Austen, c. 2 June 1832, *ibid.*, Vol. I, No. 198.

8 There is the curious case of Disraeli's involvement in a publication known as the *Gallomania*, in 1832, when he was supposedly a Radical. This was an attack on the pro-French foreign policy of the Whigs, based on documents supplied by the mysterious Baron de Haber, an agent for the reactionary Charles X, who had been deposed as King of France in the 'July revolution' of 1830. In a letter to his sister Sarah on 20 February 1832, Disraeli had written excitedly: 'Such secrets! I am writing a book which will electrify all Europe...I hope to produce something which will not only ensure my election, but produce me a political reputation, which is the foundation of everything, second to none.' *Disraeli Letters*, Vol. I, No. 140.

9   Printed in William Hutcheon (ed.), *Whigs and Whiggism: Political Writings of Benjamin Disraeli* (London, 1913), pp. 16–22.

10   Disraeli's election address, 13 June 1835; Disraeli to Beadon, 2 July and 9 August 1835, *Disraeli Letters*, Vol. II, Nos. 406, 409, 415.

11   There was indeed some similarity between Burdett's and Disraeli's thinking. Both acknowledged an intellectual debt to the Queen Anne Tory, Lord Bolingbroke. Their 'radicalism' was derived from a mythical view of the medieval constitution and of the 'historic rights' of Englishmen, rather than from Utilitarianism. See J. R. Dinwiddy, 'Sir Francis Burdett and Burdettite Radicalism', *History*, LXV (1980), pp. 17–31.

12   Hutcheon (ed.), *Whigs and Whiggism*, pp. 111–232. See also the summary in Disraeli's 'Spirit of Whiggism' (1836), *ibid.*, pp. 327–56.

13   *Ibid.*, p. 126.

14   *Ibid.*, p. 215.

15   e.g. Linda Colley, *In Defiance of Oligarchy: The Tory Party, 1714–60* (Cambridge, 1982).

16   Hutcheon (ed.), *Whigs and Whiggism*, pp. 215–18.

17   These are printed in *ibid.*, pp. 233–326; and in *Disraeli Letters*, Vol. II, Appendix 2.

18   All the same, Mary Anne was a jealous and demanding lover, and it is unlikely that Disraeli was entirely faithful to her. For one furious row over another woman (possibly Lady Londonderry), see Disraeli to his sister, Sarah, 18 July 1849, *Disraeli Letters*, Vol. V, No. 1857.

19   Disraeli to Sarah Disraeli, 16 March 1838, 26 April 1838, 10 August 1839, *ibid.*, Vol. III, Nos. 747, 766, 980.

20   Disraeli to Peel, 2 March 1838 *ibid.*, Vol. III, No. 738; Disraeli to Sarah Disraeli, 21 November 1837 and 20 May 1841, *ibid.*, Vol. II, No. 676, Vol. III, No. 1157.

21   Disraeli to Charles Attwood, 7 June 1840, *ibid.*, Vol. III, No. 1065.

22   Ian Newbould, 'Sir Robert Peel and the Conservative Party, 1832–1841: A Study in Failure?', *English Historical Review*, XCVIII (1983), pp. 550–6; Betty Kemp, 'The General Election of 1841', *History*, XXXVII (1952), pp. 155–6.

23   Disraeli to Peel, 5 September 1841, *Disraeli Letters*, Vol. III, No. 1186.

24   Disraeli to Mary Anne, 25 February 1842, *ibid.*, Vol. IV, No. 1217.

25   Disraeli to same, 23 April 1842, *ibid.*, Vol. IV, No. 1241.

26   Disraeli to same, 26 February 1842, *ibid.*, Vol. IV, No. 1219.

27   Disraeli to same, 9 and 11 March 1842, *ibid.*, Vol. IV, Nos. 1224, 1229.

28   Cf. Lord John Manners' Journal, 7 July 1842: 'perhaps there never was a house of commons in which there was so much young talent frittered away'. Charles Whibley, *Lord John Manners and his Friends* (London, 1925), Vol. I, p. 142.

29   A draft is in *Disraeli Letters*, Vol. IV, Appendix 3.

30   For this and what follows, see Richard Faber, *Young England* (London, 1987).

31   *Ibid.*, pp. 164–82, 252–6.

32   For instance, he completely changed his assessment of the 'Glorious Revolution' of 1688. In the 'Vindication' he had adopted a conventional view, denouncing the tyrannical later Stuart Kings, welcoming the revolution as a national movement (because it was supported by the Tories), and praising William III for resisting the Whigs' attempts to turn him into a Venetian Doge. Hutcheon (ed.), *Whigs and Whiggism*, pp. 137, 182–3, 207–8, 214. But in *Sybil* (Bk. I, Ch. 3), he scoffed at the idea that James II was trying to restore popery in England, and condemned William III for his legacy of Dutch Finance (i.e. the national debt) and French Wars.

33   Disraeli was careful to point out that the virtues of the medieval English Church had nothing to do with its Catholicism.

34   Disraeli to Manners, 27 October 1844, *Disraeli Letters*, Vol. IV, No. 1379.

35   See D. R. Fisher, 'Peel and the Conservative Party: The Sugar Crisis of 1844 Reconsidered', *Historical Journal*, XVIII (1975), pp. 279–302.

36   See Blake, *Disraeli*, pp. 184–9, for this and other speeches in 1845. Disraeli's allusion was to the Devon Commission, set up in 1843 to inquire into the land problem in Ireland.

37   Disraeli to the editor of the *Morning Post*, 11 August 1843, *Disraeli Letters*, Vol. IV, No. 1320.

38   Blake, *Disraeli*, pp. 225–7, 231–2, 236–9.

39   On the final night of the debate, 15 May, Disraeli made his notorious denial that he had ever sought office from Peel in 1841. It has recently been pointed out that he probably could have got away with this statement, if Peel had challenged it, on the ground that his letter of September 1841 only expressed regret at being excluded, and did not actually *ask* for office. *Disraeli Letters*, Vol. IV, p. xxxvi.

40   Disraeli to Sir George Sinclair, 13 March 1846, *ibid.*, Vol. IV, No. 1475.

41   Disraeli to Mary Anne, 29 June 1846, *ibid.*, Vol. IV, No. 1499.

42   Faber, *Young England*, p. 119.

43   *Disraeli Letters*, Vol. I, Appendix 3; Disraeli to Manners, 17 December [1845], *ibid.*, Vol. IV, No. 1455. See also Disraeli's famous character-sketch of Peel in his biography, *Lord George Bentinck* (London, 1852), pp. 303–6.

44   Faber, *Young England*, p. 185.

45   Paul Smith, 'Disraeli's Politics', *Transactions of the Royal Historical Society*, 5th Series, XXXVII (1987), pp. 65–86.

46   Blake, *Disraeli*, pp. 3–7.

2   THE MID-VICTORIAN CONSERVATIVE PARTY

1   The purchase was not completed until late in 1848, and matters were complicated by Lord George Bentinck's death. Disraeli had to persuade Bentinck's relatives to provide the necessary money, 'observing, that it wd. be no object to them & no pleasure to me, unless I played the high game in public life; & that I cd. not do that witht being on a rock.' Disraeli to Mary Anne, 18 October 1848, J. Matthews and M. G. Wiebe (eds.), *Benjamin Disraeli Letters* (University of Toronto Press, 1982), Vol. V, No. 1730.

2   Disraeli's election address, 22 May 1847, *ibid.*, Vol. IV, No. 1551.

3   For a recent reappraisal, see Angus Macintyre, 'Lord George Bentinck and the Protectionists: A Lost Cause?' *Transactions of the Royal Historical Society*, 5th Series, XXXIX, (1989), pp. 141–66.

4   Disraeli to Sarah Disraeli, 4 September 1848, *Disraeli Letters*, Vol. V, No. 1709.

5   Disraeli to Stanley, 26 December 1848, *ibid.*, Vol. V, No. 1755.

6   Disraeli to Mary Anne, 5 January 1849; Disraeli to Metternich, 25 January 1849, Disraeli to Manners, 29 January 1849, *ibid.*, Vol. V, Nos. 1761, 1778, 1781.

7   Disraeli to Mary Anne, 31 January 1849, *ibid.*, Vol. V, No. 1782.

8   Disraeli to Metternich, 13 January 1849, *ibid.*, Vol. V, No. 1769.

9   Disraeli to George Mathew, 28 August 1846, *ibid.*, Vol. IV, No. 1554; cf. Disraeli to Sarah Disraeli, 28 May 1849, *ibid.*, Vol. V, No. 1834.

10 Robert Stewart, *The Foundation of the Conservative Party, 1830–1867* (London, 1978), p. 238.

11 Disraeli to Sir George Sinclair, 29 February 1848, *Disraeli Letters*, Vol. V, No. 1633.

12 J. R. Vincent (ed.), *Disraeli, Derby and the Conservative Party: The Political Journals of Lord Stanley, 1849–69* (Hassocks, 1978), March 1850.

13 Disraeli to Lady Londonderry, 1 September 1846, *Disraeli Letters*, Vol. IV, No. 1515.

14 Disraeli to same, 12 April 1849, *ibid.*, Vol. V, No. 1811.

15 Disraeli to Sarah Disraeli, 8 March 1851, *ibid.*, Vol. V, No. 2105.

16 Stanley to Christopher, 8 January 1849, in Stewart, *Foundation of Conservative Party*, p. 234.

17 *Stanley Journals*, 25 February 1851.

18 Robert Blake, *Disraeli* (London, 1966), p. 297.

19 *Stanley Journals*, 9, 18, 25 and 28 June 1850.

20 Disraeli to Manners, 19 September 1846, *Disraeli Letters*, Vol. IV, No. 1519.

21 Disraeli to Lord Ponsonby, 9 July 1848, *ibid.*, Vol. V, No. 1664.

22 *Stanley Journals*, 26 June and 12 July 1852.

23 Disraeli to Manners, 16 October 1850, *Disraeli Letters*, Vol. V, No. 2049.

24 P. R. Ghosh, 'Disraelian Conservatism: A Financial Approach', *English Historical Review*, XCIX (1984), pp. 272–7. It is true that, the night before the fatal vote, Disraeli had a meeting with John Bright in an attempt to secure radical support for the Budget. But this was surely only a desperate last-gasp bid to avoid defeat.

25 This is a necessarily simplified account of a complex subject. See Blake, *Disraeli*, pp. 328–48, for further details. There can be little doubt that the Budget was a rushed, haphazard, and somewhat muddled measure.

26 E. M. Whitty, *St.Stephen's in the Fifties* (ed. Justin McCarthy, London, 1906), pp. 64–7 (18 December 1852).

27. Derby to Lord Londonderry, 21 December 1852, in Stewart, *Foundation of Conservative Party*, p. 261.

28 Lord Malmesbury, *Memoirs of an Ex-Minister* (London, 1884), Vol. I, p. 303 (13 February 1852).

29 On this subject generally, see Stewart, *Foundation of Conservative Party*, pp. 289–309.

30 *Stanley Journals*, 17 February 1853.

31 *Ibid.*, 10 January, 14 January and 4 April 1853.

32 *Ibid.*, 17 December 1853.

33   *Ibid.*, 23 February 1854. See also 25 January 1854.

34   *Ibid.*, 9 February, 3 March, 14 April 1853.

35   *Ibid.*, 30 June 1853.

36   *Ibid.*, 24 March 1853.

37   *Ibid.*, 24 December 1852.

38   Malmesbury, *Memoirs*, Vol. I, p. 434 (12 May 1854).

39   There is a detailed account in the *Stanley Journals*, 'Memorandum on the Change of Ministry, January–February 1855'.

40   Malmesbury, *Memoirs*, Vol. II, pp. 8–9 (12 February 1855). Cf. Sir John Pakington to Sir William Jolliffe, 5 February 1855: 'it must be Lord Derby *ere long*'. Hylton MSS (Somerset Record Office), DD/HY/24/9/109.

41   Disraeli to Malmesbury, 30 November 1855, in Malmesbury, *Memoirs*, Vol. II, pp. 37–8.

42   Stewart, *Foundation of Conservative Party*, p. 314.

43   Angus Hawkins, *Parliament, Party and the Art of Politics in Britain, 1855–59* (London, 1987), p. 47.

44   Malmesbury, *Memoirs*, Vol. II, pp. 45–6 (26 April 1856).

45   T. E. Taylor to Jolliffe, 25 November [1856], Hylton MSS, DD/HY/24/21/17.

46   Disraeli to Jolliffe, 29 April [1857], *ibid.*, DD/HY/44/c2165/62.

47   Taylor to Jolliffe, [13 December 1857], *ibid.*, DD/HY/24/21/5.

48   Hawkins, *Art of Politics*, pp. 104–6.

49   *Stanley Journals*, 21 February 1858.

50   T. A. Jenkins (ed.), *The Parliamentary Diaries of Sir John Trelawny, 1858–1865* (Royal Historical Society, Camden 4th Series, Vol. 40, 1990), 4 and 18 February 1859. A few modest gestures were also made to please the Irish MPs, and these helped to bring the Conservatives some short-term electoral gains in Ireland in 1859. See Theodore Hoppen, 'Tories, Catholics and the General Election of 1859', *Historical Journal*, XIII (1970), pp. 48–67.

51   Ghosh, 'Disraelian Conservatism: A Financial Approach', pp. 283–4.

52   Stewart, *Foundation of Conservative Party*, pp. 352–8.

53   Derby to Malmesbury, 15 December 1856, in Malmesbury, *Memoirs*, Vol. II, pp. 53–4.

54   Derby to same, 26 December 1860, *ibid.*, Vol. II, pp. 243–4.

55   P. M. Gurowich, 'The Continuation of War by Other Means: Party and Politics, 1855–1865', *Historical Journal*, XXVII (1984), pp. 621–7.

56   *Stanley Journals*, 29 January and 8 February 1861.

57   Diary, 5 and 7 June 1861, Sotheron-Estcourt MSS (Gloucester Record Office), D1571/F411.

58   Diary, 5, 12, 18–20 June 1862, *ibid.*, D1571/F412.

59   *Stanley Journals*, 6 March 1863.

60   *Ibid.*, 28 October 1863.

61   *Ibid.*, 19 February 1864.

62   *Ibid.*, 11 February 1865. See also 23 January 1862 and 19 February 1864.

63   *Ibid.*, 26 October 1865.

64   Stanley Weintraub, *Disraeli: A Biography* (London, 1993), pp. 419–36.

65   William White, *The Inner Life of the House of Commons* (ed. Justin McCarthy, London, 1897), Vol. I, pp. 5–8, (15 March and 5 April 1856).

66   *Trelawny Diaries*, 19 May 1862.

67   Whitty, *St. Stephen's in the Fifties*, pp. 259–60 (9 July 1853).

68   *Trelawny Diaries*, 17 May 1861.

69   *Ibid.*, 8–9 May 1862.

3   CONSTRUCTING THE 'TORY DEMOCRACY'

1   Figures from Robert Stewart, *The Foundation of the Conservative Party, 1830–1867* (London, 1978), p. 340.

2   Robert Blake, *The Conservative Party from Peel to Thatcher* (London, 1985), p. 46.

3   T. A. Jenkins (ed.), *The Parliamentary Diaries of Sir John Trelawny, 1858–1865* (Royal Historical Society, Camden 4th Series, Vol. 40, 1990), 7 August 1862. For Disraeli's speech, on 1 August, see W. F. Monypenny and G. E. Buckle, *The Life of Benjamin Disraeli, Earl of Beaconsfield* (London, 1929 ed.), Vol. II, p. 113.

4   26 June 1863, Monypenny and Buckle, *Disraeli*, Vol. II, p. 114.

5   See *ibid.*, Vol. II, pp. 83–114, for the whole of this section. Four of Disraeli's speeches on Church matters from this period are printed in T. E. Kebbel (ed.), *Selected Speeches of the Earl of Beaconsfield* (London, 1882), Vol. II, pp. 555–613.

6   Disraeli to Malmesbury, 22 February 1861, in Lord Malmesbury, *Memoirs of an Ex-Minister* (London, 1884), Vol. II, p. 247.

7   The issue was settled, through a bipartisan arrangement in parliament, in 1868.

8   Monypenny and Buckle, *Disraeli*, Vol. II, pp. 115–35.

9   Robert Blake, *Disraeli* (London, 1966), pp. 490–4.

10   J. R. Vincent (ed.), *Disraeli, Derby and the Conservative Party: The Political Journals of Lord Stanley, 1849–69* (Hassocks, 1978), 15 March 1869.

11   Disraeli to Malmesbury, 13 August 1852, in Malmesbury, *Memoirs*, Vol. II, p. 344.

12   One scholar has suggested that Disraeli, in the 1830s, came to see Britain as 'the destined inheritor of the civilising mission of his race. The British Empire became the translation appropriate to his needs of Jewish universalism.' Paul Smith, 'Disraeli's Politics', *Transactions of the Royal Historical Society*, 5th Series, XXXVII (1987), p. 85.

13   Disraeli had shown an interest in the idea of imperial representation in the Westminster Parliament as early as 1851, arguing that colonial MPs would tend to be allies of the Conservative Party and might therefore 'allow us to prevent... the increase of the town, or democratic, power, with[ou]t the odium of directly resisting its demands.' Disraeli to Derby, 9 and 18 December 1851, M. G. Wiebe (ed.), *Benjamin Disraeli Letters*, V (University of Toronto Press, 1993), Nos. 2205, 2209.

14   Stanley R. Stembridge, 'Disraeli and the Millstones', *Journal of British Studies*, V (1965), pp. 128–32.

15   See the unsatisfactory article by Freda Harcourt, 'Disraeli's Imperialism, 1866–1868: A Question of Timing', *Historical Journal*, XXIII (1980), pp. 87–109.

16   For the events of 1866–7, see Blake, *Disraeli*, pp. 436–47, 456–77; Stewart, *Foundation of Conservative Party*, pp. 358–66. The *Stanley Journals* are an excellent detailed source for this period.

17   i.e. the tenant paid his rent and rates to the landlord, who then paid the rates to the local authority on the tenant's behalf. In such cases, the tenant was not eligible for the vote, because it was a requirement that he should be a *direct* ratepayer.

18   William White, *The Inner Life of the House of Commons* (ed. Justin McCarthy, London, 1897), Vol. II, pp. 75–8 (17 August 1867).

19   *Selected Speeches*, Vol. II, pp. 470–89.

20   Richard Shannon, *The Age of Disraeli, 1868–1881* (London, 1992), pp. 15–23.

21   Blake, *Disraeli*, p. 486.

22   *Ibid.*, p. 508. For what follows, see Shannon, *Age of Disraeli*, pp. 52–76.

23   J. C. Lowe, 'The Tory Triumph of 1868 in Blackburn and Lancashire', *Historical Journal*, XVI (1973), pp. 733–48; R. L. Greenall, 'Popular Conservatism in Salford', *Northern History*, IX (1974), pp. 123–38, Patrick Joyce, 'The Factory Politics of Lancashire in the Later Nineteenth Century', *Historical Journal*, XVIII (1975), pp. 525–53.

24   Nancy E. Johnson, (ed.), *The Diary of Gathorne Hardy, Later Lord Cranbrook, 1866–1892* (Oxford, 1981), 20 March and 2 June 1869.

25   T. A. Jenkins (ed.), *The Parliamentary Diaries of Sir John Trelawny, 1868–1873* (Royal Historical Society, Camden 5th Series, Vol. 3, 1994), 22 April 1869.

26   *Gathorne Hardy Diary*, 28 May 1870. Cf. *Stanley Journals*, 3 March 1869.

27   *Gathorne Hardy Diary*, 26 February, 28 February, 19 May, 21 July, 11 August 1871.

28   *Trelawny Diaries*, 5 June 1871. See also 6 February 1872.

29   Lord Derby's diary, 5 February 1871, cited by Shannon, *Age of Disraeli*, p. 103.

30   *Gathorne Hardy Diary*, 3 February 1872. The fact that Lowry Corry's son, Monty, was Disraeli's private secretary suggests that the Conservative leader was probably aware of what was going on at Burghley.

31   For the friction between Disraeli and these peers, see E. J. Feuchtwanger, *Disraeli, Democracy and the Tory Party* (Oxford, 1968), pp. 3–10.

32   *Selected Speeches*, Vol. II, pp. 490–535, from which all the quotations that follow are taken. For a recent commentary, see Shannon, *Age of Disraeli*, pp. 137–42.

33   Shannon, *Age of Disraeli*, pp. 107–11.

34   See P. R. Ghosh, 'Style and Substance in Disraelian Social Reform, c. 1860–80', in P. J. Waller (ed.), *Politics and Social Change in Modern Britain* (Hassocks, 1987), pp. 59–90.

35   *Gathorne Hardy Diary*, 16 December 1872; 22 January 1873.

36   See Shannon, *Age of Disraeli*, pp. 149–52.

37   *Ibid.*, pp. 172–4.

38   Figures from Feuchtwanger, *Tory Party*, p. 81.

39   *Ibid.*, pp. 113–31.

40   Stewart, *Foundation of Conservative Party*, pp. 279–84, 325–51; Shannon, *Age of Disraeli*, pp. 118–25, 179–81.

41   Lord Derby's diary, 23 September 1873, cited by Shannon, *Age of Disraeli*, pp. 162–3.

42   Cited by Shannon, *Age of Disraeli*, pp. 180–1.

43   Blake, *Disraeli*, pp. 525–6. For a similar chance encounter between a leading Conservative and suburbia, see *Stanley Journals*, 24 April 1867.

44   Schreiber to ?, 2 July 1860, Hylton MSS (Somerset Record Office), DD/HY/24/22/5. East Surrey was a particularly tempting target for the Conservatives, since one of the sitting MPs was a prominent Radical, Peter Locke King.

45   Peek's attitudes and ambitions are of considerable interest, from the point of view of the social assimilation of the middle classes into the Conservative party. In 1864 he wrote to the Chief Whip pointing out that, in the previous sixteen years, the firm of Peek Brothers & Co. had paid some £6 million in indirect taxes — a sum equivalent to one-seventieth of the entire gross revenue of the UK Treasury during that period. His letter continued: 'With my standing as a Merchant I have every reason to be satisfied — the advancement of my only child, a boy intended for the public service, would alone induce me to wish for any higher social position'. He was therefore willing to spend a substantial amount of money to secure election to the House of Commons. At the end of his letter, Peek added: 'allow me to say that connected as I am with five or six thousand of the influential electors in all parts of the Country I am perfectly sure that the Cold shoulder given by the Conservative leaders to the Merchant & associated classes — differing so palpably from the policy of their opponents — has been very damaging: the Liberals while liberal enough in every way to their Aristocratic Connections have likewise secured the good will & co-operation of Jews, dissenters & other compact bodies... I cannot but think that a lesson might be learned out of their book not only to party but to public advantage.' Peek to Jolliffe, 2 April 1864, *ibid.*, DD/HY/24/14/11. After much pressure, Peek was eventually awarded a baronetcy by Disraeli in 1874. His son does not appear to have made much of a mark, but his grandson, the third baronet, served with distinction in the Great War.

46   *The Times*, 31 May, 17 and 21 July 1865.

47   *Ibid.*, 25 and 28 August 1871.

48   Paul Smith, *Disraelian Conservatism and Social Reform* (London, 1967), pp. 319–25.

4 PRIME MINISTER, 1874–80

1 Spofforth to Disraeli, 8 February 1874, in Richard Shannon, *The Age of Disraeli, 1868–1881* (London, 1992), p. 178.

2 On the personnel of the government, see *ibid.*, pp. 188–96; E. J. Feuchtwanger, *Disraeli, Democracy and the Tory Party* (Oxford, 1968), pp. 28–52.

3 For what follows, see Shannon, *Age of Disraeli*, pp. 223–67; Robert Blake, *Disraeli* (London, 1966), pp. 680–96.

4 Shannon, *Age of Disraeli*, p. 251.

5 H. J. Hanham, (ed.), *The Nineteenth Century Constitution* (Cambridge, 1969), pp. 66–7.

6 Nancy E. Johnson (ed.), *The Diary of Gathorne Hardy, Later Lord Cranbrook, 1866–1892* (Oxford, 1981), 9 April 1876, 6 May 1877. See also 22 April 1880.

7 Shannon, *Age of Disraeli*, pp. 294–303.

8 C. Howard and P. Gordon (eds.), *The Cabinet Journal of Dudley Ryder, Viscount Sandon* (Institute of Historical Research, 1974), 11 May 1878.

9 Blake, *Disraeli*, pp. 545–9.

10 Shannon, *Age of Disraeli*, pp. 199–205.

11 Speaker Brand's Diary, 10 August 1874, House of Lords Record Office, Hist. Coll. 95, Vol. III.

12 Henry Lucy, *A Diary of Two Parliaments* (London, 1885–6), Vol. I, pp. 68–71 (24 March 1875).

13 *Ibid.*, Vol. I, pp. 113–18 (2 August 1875).

14 *Ibid.*, Vol. I, pp. 95–6 (24 June 1875).

15 *Ibid.*, Vol. I, pp. 138–41 (5 April 1876).

16 Speaker Brand's Diary, 16 August 1876, House of Lords Record Office, Hist. Coll. 95, Vol. V.

17 For what follows, see Paul Smith, *Disraelian Conservatism and Social Reform* (London, 1967), especially ch. 5.

18 e.g. Blake, *Disraeli*, p. 543.

19 Smith, *Disraelian Conservatism*, p. 214.

20 *Ibid.*, p. 240.

21 *Ibid.*, p. 221.

22 Shannon, *Age of Disraeli*, pp. 214–15.

23 P. R. Ghosh, 'Style and Substance in Disraelian Social Reform, c. 1860–80', in P. J. Waller (ed.), *Politics and Social Change in Modern Britain* (Hassocks, 1987), pp. 71–7.

24 Smith, *Disraelian Conservatism*, p. 217.

25 See Ghosh, 'Style and Substance', p. 78, for a critique of Smith's *Disraelian Conservatism*.

26 Stanley R. Stembridge, 'Disraeli and the Millstones', *Journal of British Studies*, V (1965), p. 135.
27 *Ibid.*, pp. 135–6.
28 Blake, *Disraeli*, pp. 581–7.
29 *Ibid.*, pp. 562–3.
30 Shannon, *Age of Disraeli*, pp. 280–1.
31 For a later example, see *ibid.*, p. 396.
32 There is a detailed study by Richard Millman, *Britain and the Eastern Question 1875–1878* (Oxford, 1979).
33 Shannon, *Age of Disraeli*, p. 276.
34 See Blake, *Disraeli*, pp. 570–81, 607–10.
35 A point emphasised by P. R. Ghosh, 'Disraelian Conservatism: A Financial Approach', *English Historical Review*, XCIX (1984), pp. 289–93. The Abyssinian War of 1867–8, however, provided an indication of what was to come.
36 Cited by Shannon, *Age of Disraeli*, p. 290.
37 Derby to Salisbury, 23 December 1877, in Blake, *Disraeli*, p. 636.
38 Laurence Senelick, 'Politics as Entertainment: Victorian Music Hall Songs', *Victorian Studies*, XIX (1975), p. 169.
39 Hugh Cunningham, 'Jingoism in 1877–78', *Victorian Studies*, XIV (1971), pp. 429–53.
40 Speaker Brand's Diary, August 1878, House of Lords Record Office, Hist. Coll. 95, Vol. VIII.
41 *Sandon Journal*, 10 August 1878. For Hart Dyke's assessment, see Shannon, *Age of Disraeli*, pp. 303, 314–16.
42 See Shannon, *Age of Disraeli*, pp. 334–9.
43 *Ibid.*, pp. 367–8.
44 W. F. Monypenny and G. E. Buckle, *The Life of Benjamin Disraeli, Earl of Beaconsfield* (London, 1929 ed.), Vol. II, pp. 1386–8.
45 *Gathorne Hardy Diary*, 4 April 1880.
46 H. J. Hanham, *Elections and Party Management: Politics in the time of Disraeli and Gladstone* (2nd ed. Hassocks, 1978), p. 232.
47 Blake, *Disraeli*, p. 719.

5 DISRAELI'S ACHIEVEMENT

1 Richard Shannon, *The Age of Disraeli, 1868–1881* (London, 1992), pp. 395–6.
2 21 May 1880, in Robert Blake, *Disraeli* (London, 1966), pp. 721–2.
3 29 October 1880, in Shannon, *Age of Disraeli*, p. 412.

References

4   It is printed as an appendix to W. F. Monypenny and G. E. Buckle, *The Life of Benjamin Disraeli, Earl of Beaconsfield* (London, 1929 ed.), Vol. II.

5   J. P. Cornford, 'The Transformation of Conservatism in the Late-Nineteenth Century', *Victorian Studies*, VII (1963), pp. 35–66; Mary Chadwick, 'The Role of Redistribution in the Making of the Third Reform Act', *Historical Journal*, XIX (1976), pp. 665–83.

6   Blake, *Disraeli*, pp. 758–9; Paul Smith, *Disraelian Conservatism and Social Reform* (London, 1967), pp. 319–25.

7   Martin Pugh, *The Tories and the People, 1880–1935* (Blackwell, Oxford, 1985).

8   Disraeli to Stanley, 26 December 1848, in J. Matthews and M. G. Wiebe (eds.), *Benjamin Disraeli Letters* (University of Toronto Press, 1982-), Vol. V, No. 1755.

9   For a somewhat over-schematic argument along these lines, see Clyde J. Lewis, 'Theory and Expediency in the Policy of Disraeli', *Victorian Studies*, IV (1961), pp. 237–58.

10   For an early reference to the condition of the people, see Disraeli's Wycombe address, 1 October 1832, *Disraeli Letters*, Vol. I, No. 215.

11   T. E. Kebbel, *A History of Toryism* (London, 1886), pp. 335, 353, 370.

12   Roland Quinault, 'Lord Randolph Churchill and Tory Democracy, 1880–1885', *Historical Journal*, XXII (1979), pp. 141–65.

13   Richard Jay, *Joseph Chamberlain: A Political Study* (Oxford, 1981), pp. 172–84.

14   Monypenny and Buckle, *Disraeli*, Vol. II, pp. 1517–19.

15   Arthur Bryant, *The Spirit of Conservatism* (London, 1929), pp. 39–40; R. J. White, *The Conservative Tradition* (London, 1950), p. 15.

16   F. J. C. Hearnshaw, *Conservatism in England* (London, 1933), p. 215. Cf. Lord Henry Bentinck, *Tory Democracy* (1918), cited by Shannon, *Age of Disraeli*, p. 4.

17   Reginald Northam, '*Conservatism the Only Way*' (London, 1939), p. 82.

18   Geoffrey Butler, *The Tory Tradition* (London, 1914), pp. 67–8.

19   Hearnshaw, *Conservatism*, p. 21; White, *Conservative Tradition*, pp. 12–20.

20   Bryant, *Spirit of Conservatism*, p. 75.

21   Nigel Fisher, *Harold Macmillan* (London, 1982), pp. 6, 130–1, 339, 367–8.

22   Robert Blake, *Disraeli* (London, 1966); F. B. Smith, *The Making of the Second Reform Bill* (Cambridge, 1966); E. J. Feuchtwanger, *Disraeli, Democracy and the Tory Party* (Oxford, 1968); Stanley R. Stembridge, 'Disraeli and the Millstones', *Journal of British Studies*, V (1965), pp. 122–39; Paul Smith, *Disraelian Conservatism and Social Reform* (London, 1967).

23   Norman Gash, *Sir Robert Peel* (2 vols, London, 1961–72). It might be noted that this interpretation has, in turn, been challenged: e.g. Boyd Hilton, 'Peel: A Reappraisal', *Historical Journal*, XXII (1979), pp. 585–614.

24   Angus Hawkins, 'Lord Derby and Victorian Conservatism: A Reappraisal', *Parliamentary History*, VI (1987), pp. 280–301.

25   Ian Gilmour, *Inside Right* (London 1977), pp. 74–86.

BIBLIOGRAPHICAL NOTE

The official biography of Disraeli was written by W. F. Monypenny and G. E. Buckle: *Life of Benjamin Disraeli, Earl of Beaconsfield* (6 vols, London, 1910–20; revised 2 vol. edn, 1929), which made considerable use of his private papers. Of the many modern studies, Robert Blake's *Disraeli* (London, 1966) is outstanding. A recent addition to the literature, drawing on some fresh archive material, is by Stanley Weintraub, *Disraeli: A Biography* (London, 1993).

For the period up to 1851, Disraeli's complete correspondence is now available, in J. Matthews and M. G. Wiebe (eds.), *Benjamin Disraeli Letters* (5 vols, University of Toronto Press, 1982–93). Further instalments are eagerly awaited. Helen M. Swartz and Marvin Swartz (eds.), *Disraeli's Reminiscences* (London, 1975), is based on material written in the early 1860s. In his final years, Disraeli corresponded regularly with two female confidants, providing us with a useful source: Marquis of Zetland (ed.), *The Letters of Disraeli to Lady Bradford and Lady Chesterfield, 1873–1881* (2 vols, London, 1929).

William Hutcheon (ed.), *Whigs and Whiggism: Political Writings of Benjamin Disraeli* (London, 1913), collects together many of his pamphlets and newspaper letters from the 1830s, together with a few later pieces. There is a convenient collection of Disraeli's speeches, public and parliamentary, by T. E. Kebbel (ed.), *Selected Speeches of the Earl of Beaconsfield* (2 vols, London, 1882). The most important of Disraeli's novels are his Young England trilogy, *Coningsby or The New Generation* (1844), *Sybil or The Two Nations* (1845), and *Tancred or The New Crusade* (1847). These are available in various editions.

Some relevant material can be gleaned from the lives, letters and memoirs of Disraeli's contemporaries, including the following: Charles Whibley, *Lord John Manners and his Friends* (2 vols, London, 1925); Lord Malmesbury, *Memoirs of an Ex-Minister* (2 vols, London, 1884); Sir Arthur Hardinge, *The Life of Edward Henry Molyneux Herbert, Fourth Earl of Carnarvon* (3 vols, London, 1925); A. E. Gathorne Hardy, *Gathorne Hardy, First Earl of Cranbrook: A Memoir*

(2 vols, London, 1910); Andrew Lang, *Sir Stafford Northcote, First Earl of Iddesleigh* (2 vols, London, 1890); Lady Gwendolen Cecil, *Life of Robert, Marquis of Salisbury* (4 vols, London, 1921–32); Sir Herbert Maxwell, *Life and Times of the Right Hon. William Henry Smith MP* (2 vols, London, 1893). See also A. C. Benson and Lord Esher (eds.), *The Letters of Queen Victoria*, 1st Series, 1837–61 (3 vols, London, 1907), and G. E. Buckle (ed.), *The Letters of Queen Victoria*, 2nd Series, 1862–85 (3 vols, London, 1926–8).

The Journal kept by Lord Stanley, later the 15th Earl of Derby (the son of the Conservative Prime Minister), is of first-rate importance as a source for Disraeli's leadership of the Conservative Party. It has been edited by J. R. Vincent *Disraeli, Derby and the Conservative Party: The Political Journals of Lord Stanley, 1849–69* (Hassocks, 1978), and *The Derby Diaries, 1869–1878*, (Royal Historical Society, Camden Fifth Series, Vol. 4, 1994). Another useful record of events may be found in Nancy E. Johnson (ed.), *The Diary of Gathorne Hardy, Later Lord Cranbrook, 1866–1892*, (Oxford, 1981). On a miniature scale, there is also C. Howard and P. Gordon (eds.), *The Cabinet Journal of Dudley Ryder, Viscount Sandon, 11 May to 10 August 1878* (Institute of Historical Research, 1974).

The history of the Conservative party in the Victorian period is well covered in the secondary literature. There are detailed treatments by Robert Stewart, *The Foundation of the Conservative Party, 1830–1867* (London, 1978), and Richard Shannon, *The Age of Disraeli, 1868–1881* (London, 1992). See also Robert Blake, *The Conservative Party from Peel to Thatcher* (London, 1985), and Bruce Coleman, *Conservatism and the Conservative Party in Nineteenth Century Britain* (London, 1988).

Richard Faber, *Young England* (London, 1987) provides a sympathetic account of this movement with which Disraeli was involved in the 1840s. John Vincent, *Disraeli* (London, 1990) is a brief study of Disraeli's political ideas. An attempt to argue for an underlying continuity in Disraeli's political thinking and conduct was made some years ago by Clyde J. Lewis, 'Theory versus Expediency in the Policy of Disraeli', *Victorian Studies*, IV (1961), pp. 237–58. See also the stimulating paper by Paul Smith, 'Disraeli's Politics', *Transactions of the Royal Historical Society*, 5th series, XXXVII (1987), pp. 65–86. P. R. Ghosh, 'Disraelian Conservatism: A Financial Approach', *English Historical Review*, XCIX (1984), pp. 268–96, makes exaggerated claims for the budget of 1852, but is nevertheless useful on the way that Disraeli embraced the new Peelite Free Trade orthodoxies after he became Conservative leader in the Commons.

For the politics of the late 1850s, see Angus Hawkins, *Parliament, Party and the Art of Politics in Britain, 1855–59* (London, 1987), and K. Theodore Hoppen, 'Tories, Catholics and the General Election of 1859', *Historical Journal*, XIII (1970), pp. 48–67. There is also an important article by P. M. Gurowich, 'The Continuation of War by Other Means: Party and Politics, 1855–1865', *Historical Journal*, XXVII (1984), pp. 603–31.

There are two studies of the second Reform Act, by F. B. Smith, *The Making of the Second Reform Bill* (Cambridge, 1966), and Maurice Cowling, *1867: Disraeli, Gladstone and Revolution* (Cambridge, 1967). For the Conservative Party after 1867, E. J. Feuchtwanger, *Disraeli, Democracy and the Tory Party* (Oxford, 1968), is valuable. It can be supplemented on the electoral side of things, by H. J. Hanham, *Elections and Party Management: Politics in the Time of Disraeli and Gladstone* (2nd ed., Hassocks, 1978). Disraeli's attitude to the colonies is the subject of Stanley R. Stembridge, 'Disraeli and the Millstones', *Journal of British Studies*, V (1965), pp. 122–139. Freda Harcourt, 'Disraeli's Imperialism, 1866–1868: A Question of Timing', *Historical Journal*, XXIII (1980), pp. 87–109, argues (unconvincingly, in my view) for the importance of the Abyssinian war in the development of Disraeli's interest in empire. Paul Smith, *Disraelian Conservatism and Social Reform* (London, 1967), provides a detailed treatment, but see also the revisionist piece by P. R. Ghosh, 'Style and Substance in Disraelian Social Reform, c. 1860–80', in P. J. Waller (ed.), *Politics and Social Change in Modern Britain* (Hassocks, 1987). On foreign policy in the post-1874 period, there is Richard Millman, *Britain and the Eastern Question, 1875–1878* (Oxford, 1979), and Marvin Swartz, *The Politics of British Foreign Policy in the Era of Disraeli and Gladstone* (London, 1985).

INDEX